Saxon Army of the Austrian War of Succession and the Seven Years War:
Uniforms Organisation and Equipment

Dr Stephen Summerfield

Swiss guard in Interim (left) and Service Dress (right), 1756
[Wilhelm Dietrich, 1907]

KEN TROTMAN PUBLISHING

Published in 2011 by Ken Trotman Publishing.
Booksellers & Publishers
P.O. Box 505
Godmanchester
Huntingdon PE29 2XW
England
Tel: 01480 454292
Fax: 01480 384651
www.kentrotman.com

© Dr. Stephen Summerfield

All rights reserved. No part of this publication
may be reproduced, stored in a retrieval system or transmitted
in any form or by any means electrical,
mechanical or otherwise without first seeking the
written permission of the copyright owner and
of the publisher.

ISBN: 978-1-907417-26-9

Contents

Contents	3
Order of Battles	4
Tables	5
Preface	**6**
Acknowledgements	7
Chapter 1 Saxon Army	**8**
Chapter 2: Generals	**16**
Uniforms of Staff Officers	19
Feldjäger	21
Chapter 3: Saxon Guard	**22**
Guard Infantry	22
Guard Cavalry	32
Cadets	42
Chapter 4: Saxon Infantry (1735-63)	**43**
Saxon Infantry	47
Disbanded Infantry Regiments in 1748	68
Musketeer Uniform	70
Chapter 5: Saxon Grenadier	**79**
Grenadier Uniform	82
Chapter 6: Kreis Regiments	**91**
Chapter 7: Infantry Flags	**97**
M1732 Infantry Flags	97
M1753 Infantry Flags	99
M1758 Saxon Infantry Fags	104
Chapter 8: Saxon Cuirassier	**105**
The "Old" Cuirassier Regiments	107
Cuirassier Regiments 1732-48	114
Cuirassiers Regiments formed in 1748	118
Cuirassier Uniform	122
Chapter 9: Saxon Dragoons	**128**
Dragoon Uniforms	132
Chapter 10: Chevauleger	**135**
Chevauleger Uniform	147
Chapter 11: Polish Ulan Pulks	**149**
Ulan Uniform 1741-63	155

Chapter 12: New Saxon Cavalry Regiments (1761-63)	**158**
Reiter Regiment	158
Chapter 13 Cavalry Standards	**161**
Guard Cavalry Standards	162
Cuirassier Standards	163
Dragoon Standards	167
Chevauleger Flags	169
Ulan Standards	174
Chapter 14: Artillery	**175**
Chapter 15: Saxon Quick-Fire Guns	**178**
Geschwindstück	178
French 4pdr "*à la Suédoise*" (1757-63)	181
New M1766 Quick-Fire Guns	181
Chapter 16: Engineer Corps	**182**
Chapter 17: Garrison and Invalid Companies	**184**
Invalid Company	184
Fortress Garrison Officers (1748-63).	185
Henneberg Militia	185
Chapter 18: Saxon Sidearms	**187**
Infantry Swords	188
Polearms	188
Bibliography	**189**
Regimental Index	**191**

Order of Battles

OOB 1: *The 6,000 strong Saxon Auxiliary Corps of May 1735.*	*9*
OOB 2: *Saxon Cavalry mobilised on 29 December 1740.*	*10*
OOB 3: *Saxon Army mobilised on October 1741.*	*10*
OOB 4: *Saxon Army in 1741 of about 34,000 men*	*11*
OOB 5: *Saxon Army in 1744.*	*12*
OOB 6: *Saxon Army of 18,617 men in early 1756*	*14*
OOB 7: *Saxon cavalry regiments stationed in Poland*	*15*
OOB 8: *Guard Infantry Regiments (1733)*	*22*
OOB 9: *Guard Cavalry Regiments (1733)*	*32*
OOB 10: *Saxon infantry regiments during the War of Polish Succession.*	*43*
OOB 11: *Distribution of disbanded infantry regiments in 1748.*	*45*
OOB 12: *The Saxon Auxiliary Corps of Pinz Xaver in 11 March 1758.*	*46*
OOB 13: *Grenadier Battalions formed in 1756.*	*79*
OOB 14: *Prussian Grenadier Battalions formed in March 1756.*	*79*
OOB 15: *Headquarters and commanders of the four Kreis-Regiments.*	*91*

Tables

Table 1: Saxon Guard Infantry Regiments (1729-56). — 22
Table 2: Uniform of Saxon Infantry Regiments 1734-42. — 71
Table 3: Saxon Infantry Regiments 1742-52. — 73
Table 4: Saxon Infantry Regiments 1753-61. — 75
Table 5: Saxon Infantry Regiments 1761-78 — 77
Table 6: Saxon Infantry Grenadier caps (c1756). — 85
Table 7: Kurprinzessin wore grenadier caps and fusilier caps (c1756). — 85
Table 8: Saxon Guard Grenadier mitre caps (c1756). — 85
Table 9: The Fusilier Regiment Roccow wore the fusilier cap (1742-56). — 86
Table 10: Grenadier company uniforms (1757-60) — 87
Table 11: Saxon Circle Regiments (1733-45) — 92
Table 12: Saxon Circle Regiments (1745-63) — 94
Table 13: Summary of M1753 flags of the Saxon Garde. — 99
Table 14: Saxon M1753 infantry flags. — 100
Table 15: Cuirassier Regiments 1734-48. — 122
Table 16: Cuirassier Regiments 1748-56. — 124
Table 17: Dragoon kettledrum hangings. — 132
Table 18: Saxon Dragoon Regiments in 1735-48. — 134
Table 19: Saxon Chevauleger Regiments in 1735-41. — 147
Table 20: Saxon Chevauleger Regiments in 1742-52. — 147
Table 21: Saxon Chevauleger Regiments in 1753-63 — 147
Table 22: Saxon Ulan Pulks — 156
Table 23: M1730 standards. — 163
Table 24: Saxon Cuirassier Standards in 1745. — 164
Table 25: M1748 Cuirassier Standard. — 164
Table 26: M1752 Cuirassier Standards. — 167
Table 27: Dragoon flags in 1730. — 167
Table 28: 1745 Dragoon flags in 1746. — 168
Table 29: Chevauleger Ordinarefahne. — 169
Table 30: Saxon small-arms. — 187

Preface

In 1730, the protestant Elector of Saxony converted to Roman Catholicism to become elected as King of Poland. It is interesting that soon after the death of Augustus the Strong, the uniform coat changed from their traditional red to white so came into line with the other Catholic states of Austria, France and Spain.[1] The First and Second Silesian War or more commonly in English called the War of Austrian Succession (1740-48) put an even greater strain upon Saxony who had change sides and chose the losing side. At the start of the Seven Years War in 1756, the Saxon Army was captured by Frederick II at Pirna and forcibly enlisted in his Prussian army. The remnants that escaped fought on with the Austrians and French. In 1763, Saxony was confirmed as a third rank power with the loss of Poland.

Festung Sonnenstein, Pirna in 1755 by Canaletto

The author has decided it is best simply to present the illustrations and where possible resolve the inconsistencies. The precise details of uniforms are difficult to sort out with the distance of time and these have been highlighted rather than reconciled by the works of R.D. Pengel (1979-1981) that was based heavily upon the excellent work of Friedrich Schirmer in the 1940s supplemented Dr Martin Lange, R. Clifford and Alistair Sharman in 1981.

The pioneering work and illustrations of Rudolf Trache (1866-1948), Dr Wilhelm Dietrich (1886-65) and Richard Knötel (1857-1914) combined with the later work of Hasse and Eichhorn (1936), Johannes Eichhorn for Hans Brauer (1930s) and the Sturm cigarette cards of 1932 have been used to illustrate this book. Recently the work of R. D. Pengel (1979-1981), Wilhelm Friedrich (1998) and Stephen Manley (1998) has explored the uniforms of this fascinating army. A debt of gratitude must be made to the wonderful work of the contributors to the *Seven Years War Project* [*www.kronoskaf.com/syw*] including Dr. Marco Pagan, Christian Rogge and Franco Saudelli; Lars-Holger Thümmler of *Generalstad* [*www.kuk-wehrmacht.de*] and Vlad

---

[1] See Müller et al. (1984) *Die Armee Augusts des Starken: Das Sächische Heer von 1730-1733* for details of the earlier army of Augustus the Strong of Saxony.

Gromoboy on the Saxon army (1730-5) and Polish Ulan (1730-63) [*www.gromoboy.narod.ru/saxon/saxon.html*]

The sound advice of Andrew Brentnall with reference to Johann Edmund Hottenroth (1910) and the later work of Dr. Martin Lange (1981) gave some order to the complex area of Saxon flags and standards. In so doing he exposed many errors that otherwise would have been made.

Since writing the book on *Saxony Artillery 1733-1827*, Christian Rogge's investigations and reconstructed 1:24 scale plans based upon M1751 Sardinian version supplied by Giovanni Cerino-Badone and the Prussian M1746 Oettner 3-pdr has shed light upon the Saxon *Geschwindstück* [quick fire gun.] These are explored in more detail in *Smoothbore Ordnance Journal* Issue 4.

The following conventions have been used that conform to the previous books in this series:
- Saxon rank titles and names have been preserved as far as possible. It should be noted that there is a wide variety of spellings for names in the literature, most notably the use of "C" in Austrian literature rather than modern "K."
- Hyphens have been used on certain compound German terms to assist the non-German speakers.
- The *Chevauleger* [CL], Cuirassier [KR], Dragoon [DR], Hussar [HR], Infantry Regiments [IR], *Kreis* IR have been assigned by their seniority in 1756. Saxon Infantry in Prussian service in 1756-63 [S].
- Certain colours have been left in the German, as there is no English equivalent such as *paille* [light buff yellow] and *bleumourant* [deep sky blue].
- The Saxons used their own measurements throughout the period and these have been converted to metric.

Acknowledgements

The editorial comments of Richard Brown have been invaluable. I am grateful Andrew Brentnall, Giovanni Cerino-Badone, Gerard Cronin of Gringo 40s, Dr David Moffat, Christian Rogge, Digby Smith, Steven H. Smith, Mark Webb and Hans Karl Weiss for their kind assistance, translations and encouragement over the years. I wish to thank NGA Archive and Ken Trotman Ltd for permission to reproduce illustrations from their extensive collections. I wish to thank the British Library, Berlin Library, Copenhagen Army Museum, *Heeresgeschichtliches* Museum [HGM] in Vienna, Loughborough University Library, New York Public Library [NYPL], Rastatt Army Museum, the Royal Armouries Library at Leeds, Fort Nelson and *Sächsisches Hauptstaatarchiv* in Dresden for their kind assistance over the years.

Dr Stephen Summerfield
Loughborough University
15 October 2011.

Chapter 1
Saxon Army

On 27 June 1697, *Elector Frederick August I of Saxony* (12 May 1670–1 February 1733) at the head of his army invaded Poland following the death of Polish *King John III Sobieski* and was elected *King August II of Poland* upon converting controversially to Catholicism. Saxony had traditionally been a stronghold of German Protestantism and in consequence, it lost the prestigious leading role of the Protestant estates in the Imperial Diet to Brandenburg-Prussia.

Elector Frederick August I of Saxony (r. 1694-1733) **King August II of Poland** (r. 1697-1706 then r. 1709-1733) was born on 2 May 1670 and died 1 Feb 1733.

In 1697 he was crowned in Cracow as King of Poland and was also known as August the Strong. His illegitimate son with his mistress *Aurora von Königsmarck* was *Marshal de Saxe*.

In 1706, *Charles XII* invaded Saxony and forced *August* to yield the Polish throne by the Treaty of Altranstadt. In 1709, *King August II* returned to the Polish throne. In 1715, a revolt against *King August II of Poland* among the Polish gentry was provoked by the arbitrary acquisitions of food and fodder compounded by the murder of two Polish Officials. This was only put down with the support of the Russians in 1717. In 1720, the Russians withdrew from Poland.

On 1 February 1733, *Elector Frederick August I of Saxony* (and also *King August II of Poland*) died of alcohol poisoning in Warsaw. He was succeeded by *Frederick August II*. He inherited a strong and efficient army from his father.[2] On 5 October 1733, the *Szlachta* (Polish Parliament) under the threat from a Russian Army of 20,000, elected him as *King August III of Poland*. However, the Polish throne was contested by the popular hero *Stanislas Lesczinsky*. Five days later France declared war on Austria and started the War of Polish

---

[2] MacLagan (1981) 204

Succession.³ As King, August I was disinterested in Polish affairs and only spent less than a total of three years in Poland. Power was devolved to *Heinrich von Brühl*, who became effective dictator of Poland.⁴

By the autumn 1733, the Saxon army included five guard units, twelve infantry regiments, eight cuirassier regiments, four dragoon regiments and several *Freikorps* of different strength. The Saxon Army also included *Prunk-Kurassier*. Polish nobles wearing Polish Hussar armour and Saxon cavalry uniform. In July 1734, the Saxon army was reorganised and the regiments received new uniforms. The infantry, dragoons and cuirassiers changed their coat colour from red to white. In January 1735, Saxony supplied a Corps of 6,000 to join the Imperial army under *Prince Eugene of Savoy* in return for their assistance in Poland.⁵ They arrived on the Rhine by the end of May 1735 and returned home in January 1736.

OOB 1: The 6,000 strong Saxon Auxiliary Corps of May 1735.

Commanding officer: GL Graf Friesen
Second-in-command: GL von Diemar
Guard Brigade [*GM von Rutowski*]
    1. Garde Regiment zu Fuss and 2. Garde Regiment zu Fuss
Infantry Brigade [*GM von Kriegern*]
    von Weissenfels Regiment zu Fuss and Sachsen-Duertfurt Frei-Grenadier coy
Cuirassier Brigade
    KR1 Leib-Cuirassier Regt, "KR-iv" von Arnim, "KR-vi" von Nassau,
Artillery [*Captain Jahn*]
    6 field pieces

In 1737 Saxony negotiated a treaty to supply 7,894 men to the Imperial service against the Turks. Due to losses this was reduced to 5,565 men and they returned home in January 1740. About 6,000 men were lost for all causes.⁶ After the participation in the Turkish War in January 1740, the Saxon Army was reduced to only 20,000 effectives. It took another year to raise a further 7,800 regulars in three infantry regiments, a *Chevauleger* and a Dragoon regiment plus 8,000 militia in the four Kreis IR were raised plus numerous *Ulan Pulks* from Poland.

---

³ Zamoyski (1987) 211
⁴ In 1738, *Heinrich von Brühl* became pre-eminent advisor to the Elector and was appointed Prime Minister eight years later.
⁵ Wilson (1998) 229
⁶ Wilson (1998) 238

Saxon Army 1740-1763

On 16 December 1740, Frederick II invaded the Austrian province of Silesia.

OOB 2: Saxon Cavalry mobilised on 29 December 1740.
5,539 troopers and 2,050 horses plus 624 *Chevauleger* in Poland

Two Guard Cavalry Regiments
Garde du Corps, Garde-Karabinier
Eight Cuirassier Regiments
KR1 *Leib Cuirassier Regt*, KR2 *Königlicher Prinz*, KR3 *Vendiger*, "KR-iv" *von Arnim*, "KR-v" *Promnitz*, "KR-vi" *Nassau*, "KR-vii" *Mitwitz*, "KR-viii" *Prinz Gotha*
Four Dragoon Regiments
DR1 *von Armstädt*, DR2 *Sondershausen*. DR3 *Schlichting*, DR4 *Chevalier de Saxe*
Two Chevauleger Regiment in Poland
CL1 *Prinz Karl*, CL2 *Sybilski*

In September 1741, Saxony became allied to Bavaria, France and Prussia against Austria. A large Saxon Auxiliary Corps participated with the Franco-Bavarian Army in their successful surprise night attack on Prague on 25-26 November. In early December 1741, Charles Albert of Bavaria was proclaimed King of Bohemia. In late 1741 to early 1742, Saxon and French troops participated in the invasion of Moravia.

OOB 3: Saxon Army mobilised on October 1741.
Cavalry of 5,538 troopers with 2,050 horses, 13,612 infantry, 913 men in garrison and 8,000 men in four Kreis-Regiments.

Guard Cavalry:
Garde du Corps and *Garde-Karabinier*
Cuirassier:
KR1 *Leib-Regt*, KR2 *Königlicher Prinz*, KR3 *Vendiger*
"KR-iv" *Arnim*, "KR-v" *Promnitz*, "KR-vi" *Nassau*
"KR-vii" *Bestenbostel*, "KR-viii" *Prinz Gotha*
Dragoons:
DR1 *Arnstädt*, DR2 *Sondershausen*, DR3 *Schlichting*,
DR4 *Chevalier de Saxe*
Guard:
1st *Garde zu Fuss*, 2nd *Garde zu Fuss*, *Grenadier-Garde*
Infantry:
IR1 *Königin*, IR2 *Harthaussen*, IR3 *Caila*, IR4 *Weissenfels*,
R5 *Sulkowski*, IR6 *Kosel*, IR7 *Prinz Xaver*, IR10 *Römer*,
IR11 *Allnpeck*, Cadets (155 men plus 113 on garrison duty),
Engineers (43 men)
Garrison:
Wittenberg (337 men), Bleissenburg (111 men), Königstein (183 men) Sonnenstein (110 men), Stolpen (72 men).

OOB 4: Saxon Army in 1741 of about 34,000 men.

Infantry (35 Bns)
    1st and 2nd Garde Regiments (4 Bns)
    Garde-Grenadier Regiment (2 Bn)
    Swiss Garde (1 Bn)
    10 Line Regiments (20 Bns)
    4 *Upper Saxon Circle Infantry Regiments* (8 Bns)
    8 Garrison companies

Cavalry (52 squadrons in 16 cavalry regiments)
    Garde du Corps (6 Sq)
    Karabinier-Garde (4 Sq)
    8 *Cuirassier Regiments* (24 Sq)
    3 *Dragoon Regiments* (9 Sq)
    3 *Chevauleger Regiments* (9 Sq)

Artillery
    Artillery Regiment of 5 companies

The subsequent peace treaty of 28 July 1742 ceded Prussia the former Austrian province of Silesia and left Saxony without any territorial gains. The disillusioned *von Brühl* worked to put together an anti-Prussian alliance. In 1743 the Saxon Army including Kreis troops totalled 45,323 men.

Elector Frederick August II of Saxony (*r 1733-63*), **King August III of Poland** (*r. 1734-63*) was born on 17 Oct 1696 and died 5 Oct 1763.

In 1719, he married Maria Josepha (1699-1757) who was the daughter of *Joseph I*, the Holy Roman Emperor.

In December 1743, Saxony concluded an alliance with Austria and changed sides. As a result, in August 1744 Prussia marched through Saxony to invade Bohemia.[7]

---

[7] Hochedlinger (2003) 257

Saxon Army 1740-1763

OOB 5: Saxon Army in 1744.[8]

36 squadrons and 32 battalions split into four *Generalate* [headquarters]

Army Headquarters in Dresden
Commander in Chief: GFM Herzog zu Sachsen-Weissenfels
Inspector of Cavalry: GM von Dürrfeld
Inspector of Infantry: GM von Rochow

I Generalate - Torgau
Governor: General von Hof zu Wittenberg
Staff: GL von Birkholz, GM von Arnstädt and GM Graf Kosel
 Cavalry: DR3 *Schlichting* (2 sq in Ludau), DR *Pirch* (2 sq in Grimma), DR1 *Rechenberg* (2 sq in Pretzch), KR1 *Leib-Cuirassier* (2 sq in Oschatz)
 Infantry: *2. Garde* IR Herzberg, IR2 *Frankenberg* in Leipzig, IR6 *Graf Kosel* in Torgau, IR8 *Graf Brühl* in Lübben,

II Generalate - Bautzen
Governor: General Graf Rutowski
Staff: GL von Jazmund and GM von Arnim
 Cavalry: CL *Rutowski* (4 sq in Grossenhain), "KR-vi" *Minkwitz* (2 sq in Camenz)
 "KR-v" *O'Byrn* (2 sq in Muskau)
 Infantry: *Leib-Grenadier-Garde* in Dresden, IR1 *Königin* in Görlitz, IR5 *Sulkowski* in Bautzen, IR12 *Bellegarde* in Döbeln

III Generalate - Chemnitz
Governor: General Chevalier de Saxe
Staff: GL von Polenz, GM von Grumblow and GM du Caila
 Cavalry: *Garde du Corps* (4 sq Dresden), KR3 *Maffey* (2 sq in Freiberg) "KR-vii" *Bestenbostel* (2 sq Weida), "KR-viii" *Gersdorf* (2 sq in Reichenbach)
 Infantry: IR3 *Niesemeuschel* in Freiberg, IR10 *Römer* in Zwickau, IR11 *Allnpeck* in Schneeberg, Fus. Regt. *Schönberg* in Chemnitz

IV Generalate - Raummburg
Governor: General von Diemar
Staff: GL Graf von Renard, GM Graf Brühl and GM von Harthausen
 Cavalry: DR *Prinz Sondershausen* (2 sq in Cölleda), *Karabinier* (4 sq in Zeite), KR2 *Königlicher Prinz* (2 sq in Merseburg), "KR-iv" *Haudring* (2 sq in Sangerhausen)
 Infantry: *1 Garde* IR in Borna, IR4 *Weissenfels* in Langersalza, IR7 *Prinz Xaver* in Raumburg, IR9 *Stolberg* in Eisleben.

In Poland
Governor: GM von Sybilski
 Cavalry: CL1 *Prinz Carl* (4 sq), CL2 *Sybilski* (4 sq) and 23 *Fahnen Ulan*.

---

[8] Vollmer (2002) 34-35

In January 1745, the Quadruple Alliance of Warsaw was signed by Austria, Britain, the Dutch Republic and Saxony. In return for British and Dutch subsidies, Saxony agreed to provide 30,000 men for the defence of Bohemia. On the 29 May 1745, the Saxon Corps had 25,121 men (18 battalions and 24 squadrons) with 52 artillery pieces.[9] The superior Austro-Saxon Armies were defeated at Hohenfriedberg (4 June), Soor (30 Sept) and finally at Kesselsdorf (15 Dec) where the devastating fire of the Saxon *Geschwindstück* almost stopped the Prussian advance. The result of the series of defeats was the surrender of Dresden, the capital of Saxony and on 25 December 1745, Maria Theresa of Austria recognised Silesia as Prussian territory.[10] The resulting peace conditions were humiliating and Saxony was forced to pay an indemnity of 1 million *Thaler* to Prussia. After the Second Silesian War, the Saxon army suffered from neglect at the hands of Prime Minister Heinrich Graf von Brühl forcing 378 officers to resign.[11] The Saxon army underwent severe reductions in 1748 and then again in 1753.

In 1756, Saxony entered into an anti-Prussian alliance with Austria, Russia and Sweden. Prussia made a pre-emptive invasion of Saxony on 29 August 1756 and entered Dresden on 9 September.[12]

The ill-prepared Saxon Army retired to the armed camp of Pirna situated between Dresden and the Bohemian border. The fortresses of Pirna and Königstein secured the northern and southern ends of the position. By 10 September, the Saxon army was blockaded and this position had become a prison.

Finally on 14 September, FM von Browne commanding a 40,000 strong Austrian Army marched to relieve Pirna. On 21 September he sent Major de Martagne of the Saxon *Leibgarde* into Pirna with a plan to break the beleaguered army out of their confinement. On 28 September, his plan was accepted and the Saxons agreed to build a pontoon bridge across the Elbe on the night of 11-12 October.[13]

On the evening of 12 October, the Saxons constructed a bridge of 42 pontoons across the Elbe just above Thürmsdorf that was completed by 3 pm the next day.[14] The passage was completed by 3 pm the next day. The

---

[9] 36x 3-pdr M1734 *Geschwindstück*, 8x M1730 Heavy 6-pdrs, 4x 12pdrs and 4x 24-pdr howitzers [Kretschmar (1888) 30]
[10] Hochedlinger (2003) 258-259
[11] Mollo (1977) 60
[12] Wilson (1998) 264
[13] Duffy (2008) 21
[14] Duffy (2008) 33

Saxon Army was by now without supplies, and trapped in the loop of the River overlooked by Königstein Fortress. They were just 10 km from Field Marshal von Browne's Austrian with two rapidly forming Prussian Corps in their path. On 14 October, the Saxon commanders unanimously agreed to surrender their starving army and this was concluded on 16 October with Elector August II permitted to leave for Warsaw. FM von Browne retreated and reached his camp at Budin on 19 October.[15]

The army made an unsuccessful attempt to break-out but were forced to surrender on the 16 October to avoid starving to death. Ten line regiments, the Garde du Corps, the Rutowski Dragoons[16] and all seven of the Cuirassier regiments were captured.

OOB 6: Saxon Army of 18,617 men in early 1756

Infantry (27 Bns)
    Garde Regiments (3 Bns), 12 Line Regiments (24 Bns)
    4 Upper Saxon Circle Infantry Regiments (Cadre only)
    8 Garrison companies
Cavalry (44 squadrons in 11 cavalry regiments)
    Garde du Corps (4 Sq), *Karabinier-Garde* (4 Sq)
    5 Cuirassier Regiments (20 Sq), 4 *Chevauleger* Regiments (16 Sq)
Artillery
    Artillery Regiment of 5 companies
    Engineer Corps

Between 17 and 19 October, Frederick II incorporated Saxon regiments into Prussian service to fight against their Austrian Allies. The Saxon Cavalry was used to reinforce the Prussian cavalry and the ten Saxon infantry regiments were taken entirety. Seven of these were disbanded within a year due to heavy desertion. The remainder became Prussian 54-56 Fusilier Regiments.[17] Only the four cavalry regiments and two Tartar Pulks stationed in Poland avoided that fate.[18]

The fortress of Königstein including the men from Sonnenstein were exempted from the surrender and declared neutral for the duration of the war. The Saxon army's flags and standards were placed there and were not claimed as trophies of war. The other garrison troops were forcibly enlisted in the Prussian army along with the rest of the Saxon units.

---

[15] Duffy (2008) 31-36
[16] Also known as *Rutowski Chevauleger*. Mounted on German rather than Polish horses.
[17] Mollo (1977) 60
[18] Wilson (1998) 270

The four regiments of the electoral Saxon contingent of the Upper Saxon Circle perished with the army in 1756 and they were not raised again during the war. The Leib-Grenadier-Garde Regiment who refused to swear allegiance to Frederick II of Prussia spent the rest of the war in the neutral fortress of Königstein.

The Karabinier-Garde and the three *Chevauleger* Regiments were in Poland when the rest of the Saxon army capitulated and so avoided their fate and joined the Austrians. They were considered among the best cavalry at the disposal of the Austrians and the *Chevauleger* were copied by them.

OOB 7: Saxon cavalry regiments stationed in Poland

Karabinier-Garde Regiment
3 *Chevauleger* Regiments
2 *Ulan* Pulks [876 men]

The Saxons that had escaped the Prussians were collected in Bohemia in 1756-57 and later Hungary. In October 1757, these *Reverenten* mustered 7,331 men in twelve infantry regiments (15 Bns) organised into two brigades. On 11 March 1758, the Saxon Auxiliary Army of 10,000 men was taken into French service.[19] The Saxon Auxiliary Corps marched through southern Germany and had assembled in Strasbourg by July 1758, joining Contades Army in Westphalia by September 1758. The Saxon contingent first saw action at Lutterberg (10 Oct 1758), where its determined attacks decided the day for the French army. The Saxon Army of 9,000 men in twelve Saxon infantry regiments (15 battalions) fought at Minden (17 Aug 1759) and on 31 July 1760 took Kassel while Du Muy's Army was defeated at Warburg. Saxony remained in Prussian hands until the Peace of Hubertusburg (15 Feb 1763).

Although Saxony had not lost any territory, the Seven Years War had been as bad a disaster as the Thirty Years War. Prussia had extracted 48 million Thalers in contributions. Prime Minister von Brühl lost his political power and the office of prime minister was abolished. Thomas von Fritsch became the most influential Saxon politician and promoted economic reconstruction with the reduction of state debt. Heinrich von Brühl died in 1763. Frederick Christian, son of Frederick August II died the same year. Frederick August III was a minor, so his uncle Xaver was appointed regent (1763-1768). Frederick August III came of age in 1768.

---

[19] Wilson (1998) 268

Chapter 2: Generals

Generals did not have a prescribed uniform in the first decades of the 18th century. Saxon generals wore a red coat, richly embroidered in gold and possibly silver that was typical for state clothes of the European nobility. It was more common for generals to wear the uniform of the regiment for which he was the *Inhaber*. In 1724, France introduced a uniform for generals and Saxony was among the first of the European states to follow them on 1 February 1735. Regulation of the uniforms of generals was regulated by Austria in 1751, Bavaria in 1774 and Prussia in 1803.[20]

Uniform of Generals (1735-46)

On 7 February 1735, Saxon generals were directed to wear white coats as had also been introduced for the infantry and cavalry. However, many generals still wore the uniform of their *Inhaber* regiment.

HEADWEAR: The hat was trimmed in gold with either straight or curved edging [*point d'Espagne*]. The white plumage was of ostrich feathers.

COAT: White coat with red cuffs and turnbacks. The rank of the general was evident from the decoration of the coat and the waistcoat, which became richer the higher the rank.

General-Major [GM] had smooth gold braid.

General-Lieutenant [GL] coat had golden embroidery and buttonholes. The seams were without trimming.

General-en-Chef and *General-Feld-Marschall* [FM] had the richest embroidery. The edges of the skirts, lapels, seams, pocket tabs and waistcoat were richly embroidered with sequins.

WAISTCOAT: Red waistcoat embroidered in gold.

LEGWEAR: Red breeches, white gaiters and black shoes.

HORSE FURNITURE: Red velvet saddlecloth richly embroidered in accordance with the taste of the general.

Uniform of Generals (1747-52)

The General-Order of 29 March and 14 April 1747 specified the trimming of the uniforms of the generals as gold. The last *Generalfeldmarschall* was Herzog Johann Adolph II von Weissenfels died in 1746 and it was not until 1749 that Friedrich August Graf Rutowski (1702-64)[21] was appointed.

---

[20] Friedrich (1998) 10
[21] He was the illegitimate son of August the Strong.

General-Major, General-Lieutenant and General-zu-Fuss
1735-53

HEADWEAR: The hat was trimmed in gold with either straight or curved edging [*point d'Espagne*]. The white plumage was of ostrich feathers.

COAT: White coat with red cuffs and turnbacks. The rank of the general was evident from the decoration of the coat and the waistcoat, which became richer the higher the rank.

  General-Major [GM] had smooth gold braid on six buttonholes as well as three on the pocket flaps and three under it on the enclosed lapel.

  General-Leutnant [GL] wore a white coat that had six to eight button loops. There were three loops on the pocket flaps.

  General en Chef (and the *General-Feld-Marschall* [FM] from 1749) had six to eight button loops plus an embroidered neckline, front edges, sleeves, sleeve seams, the back, lapels and the pocket flaps.

WAISTCOAT: Red waistcoat embroidered in gold. *General-Major* [GM] had a red waistcoat with double gold braid including the pocket flaps. *General en Chef* and *General-Feld-Marschall* [FM] had a poppy red waistcoat with double braid and pocket flaps enclosed with three loops.

LEGWEAR: Red breeches, white gaiters and black shoes.

HORSE FURNITURE: Red velvet saddlecloth richly embroidered in accordance with the taste of the general.

General zu Pferd
1735-53

Uniforms of Generals 1753-66

On 10 February 1753, the coat changed from white to poppy red for generals.

HEADWEAR: Tricorn with white plume.

The *General-Major* [GM] and the

General-Leutnant [GL] had smooth golden braid.

The *General en Chef* had curved braid.

COAT: Poppy red [*ponceaurot*] coat with gold embroidered edging. *Generalmajor* [GM] had heavy gold braid on the collar, the coat front edges, the pocket flaps and the edges of the turnbacks. *General-Leutnant* [GL] still had a wide and narrow gold braid on the coat front edges and the turnback edges, but not on the collar.

CUIRASS: A cuirass was worn under the coat when generals were mounted on horses.

WAISTCOAT: Light buff [*paille*] waistcoat with gold braid.

LEGWEAR: White breeches and black long cavalry boots.

1753
Generalleutnant
Generalmajor
General

Uniforms of Staff Officers

On 7 February 1735, adjutants and general staff were directed to wear white coats that had also been introduced for the Saxon infantry and cavalry. The cuffs, turnbacks and waistcoats were red embroidered in silver. The General-Order of 29 March and 14 April 1747 specified the trimmings of the *General-Adjutant* [general's adjutant], the *Exerzitien-Meister* [exercise master], and *Brigade-Major* and the *Flügel-Adjutant* [aide-de-camp] as silver.

HEADWEAR: The hats were enclosed with all with smooth silver braid.

COAT: White coat with the following distinctions.

Aide-de-camps of *Generals en Chef* with the rank of captain had six buttons (1:2:3) with embroidered loops.

Adjutants of generals with the rank of second lieutenants had ten buttons (2:2:2:2:2) with buttonhole lace.

Exerzitien-Meister and *Brigade Major* had eight buttons with embroidered loops (2:2:2:2), on every lapel and every pocket flap three, four behind on the coat (two on every side) below the waist and a double loop on every side about the folds.

WAISTCOAT: All staff officers -wore a red waistcoat with silver braid.

Saxon Army 1740-1763

BUTTONS: Silver.
LEGWEAR: Red breeches, white gaiters and black shoes.

Feld-Jäger and General-Major, 1735-66

Saxon Army 1740-1763

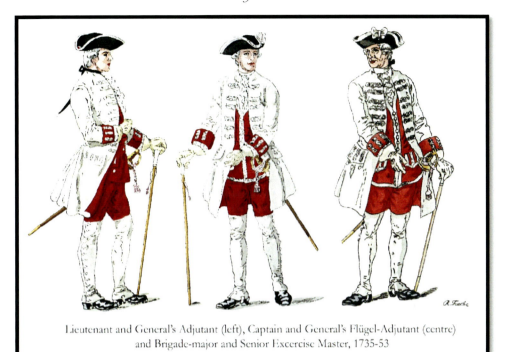

Lieutenant and General's Adjutant (left), Captain and General's Flügel-Adjutant (centre) and Brigade-major and Senior Excercise Master, 1735-53

Feldjäger, 1744 [after Trache]

Feldjäger

Formed from gamekeepers and hunters. These often acted as mounted guides and messengers.

HEADWEAR: Black tricorn had silver hat lace, white cockade and silver button.
STOCK: Black stock.
COAT: Grey coat with green collar, lapels, cuffs and turnbacks.
LACE: Silver lace to collar, cuffs and buttonholes.
BUTTON: White metal (2:2:2)
AIGUILLETTE: White with silver tassel.
LEGWEAR: Straw breeches, white boot stockings and black boots.
EQUIPMENT: Brown cartouche without decorations.
SIDEARM: Sword with brass fittings and a rifled carbine.
HORSE FURNITURE: Green saddlecloth and pistol covers with white edging.

Chapter 3: Saxon Guard

Guard Infantry

OOB 8: Guard Infantry Regiments (1733)

I-II/*1st Garde IR*
I-II/*2nd Garde IR*
I-II/*Leib-Grenadier-Garde*
I/*Janissary Battalion*
1 coy/*Schweizer Garde* [a palace guard unit]

Table 1: Saxon Guard Infantry Regiments (1729-56).

Regiment	Coat	Facings	Buttons	Pom-pom
1729-39				
1st Garde IR	yellow	red with white lace	brass	yellow
2nd Garde IR	yellow	red with white lace	white metal	yellow
Leib-Grenadier-Garde IR	red	yellow	white metal	-
Swiss Guard	white	scarlet with white blue lace	white metal	blue over yellow
1740-48				
1st Garde IR	white	red with white lace	brass	yellow
*2nd Garde (to 1748)*22	white	red with white lace	white metal	yellow
Leib-Grenadier-Garde Regt.	red	buff	white metal	-
Swiss Guard	white	scarlet with white-blue lace	white metal	blue over yellow
1748-56				
Garde IR	white	red with white lace	brass	yellow
Leib-Grenadier-Garde Regt.	red	buff	white metal	-
Swiss Guard	white	scarlet with white-blue lace	white metal	blue over yellow

---

[22] Amalgamated with 1st Garde in 1748.

Saxon Army 1740-1763

Schweizer Garde.

Schweizer Garde (Swiss Guard) was a palace guard unit created in 1725. It consisted of a single company of 129 men.

1 *Kapitän*, 1 *Kapitän-Lt*, 1 *Leutnant*, 1 *Unter-Leutnant*, 1 *Fahnrich*, 2 adjutants,
1 *Wachtmeister-Lt*, 1 *Fahnen-Junker*, 1 *Feldscher*, 6 *Rittmeister* (NCO's), 3 *Flautists*,
3 drummers, 4 *Oboists*, 4 *Zimmermann*, 96 *Trabant*.

German Uniform
HEADWEAR: Tricorn with white edging and sky blue-yellow plumes.
STOCK: White ruff.
COATS: Yellow coat with sky blue collar, cuffs and turnbacks.
WAISTCOAT: Sky blue waistcoat.
LEGWEAR: Sky blue breeches, white gaiters, black shoes.
SIDEARMS: Short sword and musket.

Trabant 1746

Officer 1746

Trabant in German uniform, *Surtout* and *Mantel*, 1756

Swiss Guard in German uniform, 1746-56 [Brauer]

Saxon Army 1740-1763

Trabant in Gala Uniform

Drummer

Swiss Guard in *Gala* uniform, 1750-56 [Brauer]

Gala Uniform

HEADWEAR: Tricorn with white edging and plumes.

STOCK: White ruff.

COATS: Yellow and sky blue jacket with white lacing.

LEGWEAR: Yellow-sky blue breeches, sky blue stockings, shoes.

SIDEARMS: Halberd and sword.

Swiss Guard in Gala Uniform, 1756
[Wilhelm Dietrich, 1907]

18th Century Swiss Guard Polearms
[After Wilhelm Dietrich, 1907]

(1st) Garde zu Fuss

Raised in 1663. In 1680 entitled Leib-Regiment and then *Leib-Garde* in 1692. When it absorbed the 2nd (Polish) *Garde* in 1703 it became known as the *Garde zu Fuss*. In 1712 it was officially entitled 1st Garde IR but was more commonly known as the *Garde zu Fuss*.

In 1756, the regiment of 1,160 men had two battalions with ten musketeer companies of 95 men each, two grenadier companies of 97 men and a regimental staff with 17 men. In 1758, as part of the Saxon Auxiliary Corps in French service, it was reformed into a single battalion of four companies plus one company from the former Leib-Grenadier-Garde serving as grenadiers. In 1763, it was reformed in three battalions with fourteen companies. In 1764 it was reduced to two battalions with ten companies when it became known as the IR Kurfürst.

Inhaber
1663 *Brandt*
1676 *Kuffe*
From 1680 *King of Poland, Elector of Saxony*

Regimental Name
1680 *Leib-Regiment*
1696 *Garde zu Fuss*
1697 *Sächsische Garde*
1701 *Deutsche Garde*
1702 *Leib-Garde zu Fuss*
1706 *Garde zu Fuss*
1712 *1st Garde zu Fuss*
1748 *Garde zu Fuss*[23] [Disbanded 1756]
1756 Prussian *S52* [Disbanded in 1763]
1758 [New]*Garde zu Fuss*
1764-1806 *Kurfürst*

Commander
1745 *Oberst von Gersdorf*
1750 *Oberst von Winkelmann*
1757-64 *Oberst-Lt von Götz*[24]

---

[23] 1st and 2nd Garde zu Fuss were amalgamated in 1744 according to Manley (1998) 21.
[24] *Oberst* in 1759.

Saxon Army 1740-1763

1st Garde zu Fuss
1742-44

Uniform (1742-53)
HEADWEAR: Black tricorn with white lace and white-red pom-pom.
GRENADIER: Prussian style Grenadier mitre.
STOCK: Red
COAT: White coat.
COLLAR and CUFFS: Red
LAPELS: none
TURNBACKS Red
WAISTCOAT: Red
LEGWEAR: Red until 1745 then white or buff.

Drummer, standard bearer and guardsman of the 1st Garde IR
1735-56

Saxon Army 1740-1763

Garde zu Fuss
1753-60

Uniform (1753-60)
GRENADIER: Black tricorn laced white.
UNIFORM: As above.

Uniform (1761-1765)
HEADWEAR: Black tricorn laced white.
GRENADIER: Austrian style bearskin.
STOCK: Red
COAT: White coat.
COLLAR and CUFFS: Red.
LAPELS: Red.
TURNBACKS Red.
WAISTCOAT: Red.

Campaign History
The regiment participated in the Rhine and Moselle Campaigns (1673-78). It fought at Vienna (1783), the siege of Ofen in Hungary (1686), in Lifland and Poland (1700-06), in Flanders (1708-12) and in Pomerania (1715). It fought against the Turks (1717-18).

War of Polish Succession. The regiment campaigned in Poland (1733) and the Rhine (1735).

War of Austrian Succession. Campaigned in Bohemia, Moravia, Silesia and Saxony (1741-2 and 1744-45). They were awarded the honour to play the Grenadiermarsch for their brave conduct at Hohenfriedberg (1745).

Seven Years War. In 1756, surrendered at Pirna and was forced into Prussian service as Prussian S52 von Blanckensee. In 1757 the regiment was reformed from Referenten in Hungary before operating with the French until 1763 being present at Lutterberg (1758), Bergen (1759), Minden (1759) and Langensalza (1761).

Saxon Army 1740-1763

2nd Garde zu Fuss

2nd Garde zu Fuss
1742-44

Amalgamated with the 1st Garde zu Fuss in 1748.

Uniform (1735-48)
HEADWEAR: Black tricorn with white lace and white-red pom-pom. Grenadiers wore the Prussian style mitre.
STOCK: Red
COAT: White coat.
COLLAR and CUFFS: Red
LAPELS: None
TURNBACKS Red
WAISTCOAT: Red
LEGWEAR: Red or buff breeches

Sergeant and officer of the 2nd Garde IR. 1735-44 [Trache]

Leib-Grenadier-Garde Regiment

Raised in 1729 as the Grenadier-Garde from drafts from the other Saxon infantry regiments by King August II of Poland. In 1734, the Leib-Grenadier-Garde totalled 1,512 men, with a regimental staff and 12 grenadier companies.

Regimental staff (28 men):
1 *Oberst*, 2 *Oberst-Lieutenante*, 2 *Majore*, 1 *Regiments-Quartiermeister*, 2 adjutants, 1 *Auditeur* (*Gerichtsoffizier*), 1 *Regiments-Feldscher*, 1 Regimental drummer, 16 *Hautboisten*, 1 *Regiments-Knecht*.

Company (123 men):
1 *Kapitän*, 1 *Premierleutnant*, 2 *Sous-Leutnante*, 3 sergeants, 1 *Fahnen-Junker*, 1 *Kapitän des Armes* (*Unterfuhrer*), 1 *Fourier*, 1 *Feldscher*, 6 corporals, 3 drummers, 1 *Querpfeifer*, 2 *Zimmerleute*, 100 grenadiers.

In 1737, the regiment was renamed the *Königliche Leibgarde zu Fuss* [Royal Foot Life Guards] and received a new uniform with sky blue facings. In 1743 renamed *Leib-Grenadier-Garde*. In January 1746 after the battle of Kesseldorff, the regiment absorbed the *Hubertusburg Grenadier Company* and the *Graf Promnitz Frei-Grenadier-Company*.

In 1756, the regiment had fourteen grenadier companies formed in two battalions of 1,684 men. It was captured at Pirna in 1756 and was not reformed. In 1757, the grenadiers served as the grenadier companies of *Garde IR*, *IR6 Prinz Maximilian* and *IR Prinz Joseph* in the Saxon auxiliary corps in French service. The regiment was not reformed until after the Peace of Hubertusburg. It reformed into three Battalions of fourteen companies. In 1764 it was reduced to two battalions of ten companies.

Inhaber
From 1729 the current *Kurfürst* or *König*

Regimental Name
1729 *Garde Grenadier-Regiment*
1733 *Grenadier-Garde-Regiment*
1737 *Königliche Leibgarde zu Fuss* [Royal Foot Life Guards]
1743 *Leib-Grenadier-Garde Regiment* [Disbanded in 1756]
1763-1806 [New] *Leib-Grenadier-Garde Regiment*

Commander
1753-63 GM *Graf zu Solms*

Garrison
From 1729: I battalion in Poland and II battalion in Meissen in Saxony.

Uniform 1737-41
Black tricorn edged yellow. White coat with sky blue facings and brass buttons.

Saxon Army 1740-1763

Lieutenant, corporal and guardsman of the Leib-Garde zu Fuss, 1738-41

Drummer and trumpeter of the Leib-Garde zu Fuss, 1738-41

Saxon Army 1740-1763

Uniform 1742-56:
HEADWEAR: Fusilier style cap.[25]
COAT: Red coat with yellow facings and
BUTTONS: White metal buttons.
LEGWEAR: Yellow breeches, white gaiters and black shoes.

Campaign History
War of Polish Succession: I battalion participated in the 1733-1735 campaigns in Poland.

War of Austrian Succession: I battalion was actively part of the 1741-42 campaigns and the entire regiment in 1744-45.

Seven Years War: In 1756 it was captured at Pirna (15 Oct) and the men were distributed among the Prussian infantry as they refused to swear an oath to the King of Prussia. It was not reformed until 1763.

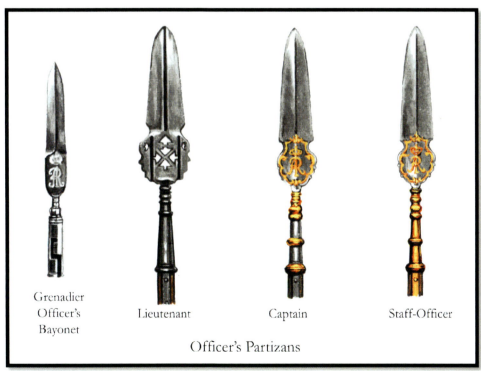

Grenadier Officer's Bayonet | Lieutenant | Captain | Staff-Officer

Officer's Partizans

---

[25] See p85-90 for details of the grenadier caps.

Guard Cavalry

August III inherited a large and expensive Guard Cavalry. He disbanded the *Chevalier-Garde* in 1733 shortly after the death of August the Strong. The Prussian Garde du Corps was modelled upon the Saxon Grand-Mousquetairs rather than the Garde du Corps.[26]

OOB 9: Guard Cavalry Regiments (1733)

1 sq/*Chevalier-Garde* [27]
1 sq/*Grand Mousquetairs* [28]
I-VI/*Garde du Corps*,
I-VI/*Karabinier-Garde*

In 1735, he disbanded the *Grand Mousquetairs Squadron* and the *Karabinier-Garde Regiment* that were amalgamated with the Garde du Corps.

Trabant of the *Garde du Corps* in *Exerzier Kollett*, 1745-1756 [Brauer]

---

[26] Schirmer (1989) II-8
[27] An elite ceremonial troop raised from Saxon nobles
[28] An elite ceremonial troop raised in Poland

Garde du Corps

Raised in 1620. Renamed the *Garde du Corps* in 1701. The *Garde du Corps* consisted of the regimental staff and six squadrons each of two companies with a total strength of 883 men during the Polish War of Succession.

Regimental staff (19 men): 2 *Oberst*, 2 *Oberst-Lt*, 2 *Majore*, 1 *Regiments-Quartiermeister*, 2 Adjutants, 1 *Auditeur*, 2 *Regiments-Feldscher*, 1 kettle-drummer, 4 trumpeters, 1 provost, 1 servant.

1st Company (73 men): 1 *Rittmeister*, 2 *Premier-Lt*, 1 *Sous-Leutnant*, 1 *Kornet*, 1 *Wachtmeister*, 1 *Fahnen-Junker*, 1 Fourier, 1 *Feldscher*, 3 corporals, 1 trumpeter and 60 *Trabanten*

2nd Company (73 men): 1 *Rittmeister*, 1 *Premier-Leutnante*, 1 *Kornet*, 1 *Wachtmeister*, 1 *Fahnen-Junker*, 1 Fourier, 1 *Feldscher*, 3 corporals, 1 trumpeter, 60 *Trabanten*

During the Austrian War of Succession, the *Garde du Corps* had an establishment of 649 troopers, larger than the other cavalry regiments. In 1741-45, they wore a cuirass on campaign.

Trabant 1738-41

Trabant in campaign dress 1741-45

Garde du Corps 1738-45 [Brauer]

Saxon Army 1740-1763

The regiment capitulated in 1756 to the Prussians. In 1763, two companies of the *Reiter* Regiment [also known as the Schleiben Cuirassier] formed a cadre for the new *Garde du Corps* that in 1812 was destroyed in Russia.

Regimental Name
1620 *Hof-Fahne* [Court Banner]
1631 *Leib-Kompagnie Einspänniger*
1681 *Leib-Trabanten-Garde zu Pferde*
1686 *Garde-Trabanten zu Ross*
1692 *Garde du Corps*
1693 *Leib-Garde-Trabanten zu Ross*
1699 *Leibgarde zu Pferde*
1701 *Trabanten-Garde zu Ross*
Oct 1701 *Garde du Corps* [29]
1704 *Garde zu Pferde*
1705 *Garde du Corps*
1707 *Garde zu Pferde*
1710-1756 *Garde du Corps* [30]
1763-1812 [New]*Garde du Corps* [31]

Chef
1740 GM *Chevalier de Saxe* [resigned in 1763]

Commander
1734 GM *von Polen* [d. 1752]
1752 GM *Graf Vitzthum von Eckstädt*
1763 GM *von Winckelmann*.

Uniform
The Garde du Corps had three different uniforms: a full (parade) dress, an *Interim* (undress/campaign) and an *Exerzier* [exercise] uniform. The regiment did not wear cuirass.

Full (Parade) Dress
HEADWEAR: Black tricorn with golden braid, button, and white cockade.
STOCK: White stock.
COAT: *Paille Kollet* with red collar, cuffs and lapels with gold lace.
WAISTCOAT: Red waistcoat with gold lace.
SUPERVEST: Red tabard with a large emblem on the breast of a gold star with a Polish white eagle, "AR" cipher and crown on a red background.
LEGWEAR: *Paille* breeches and black long cavalry boots.

---

[29] Absorbed the *Grand-Musketärs, Karabinier* and *Grenadiers zu Pferde*
[30] Oct 1756 Capitulated to the Prussians at Pirna
[31] The regiment was destroyed in Russia in 1812.

Saxon Army 1740-1763

EQUIPMENT: White belts.

Garde du Corps in full dress uniform, 1748-56 [after Trache]

Officers
HEADWEAR: Tricorn with gold braid, button loop and white feathers.
SUPERVEST: Red tabard with gold lace on the collar, around the sleeve holes. The large emblem on the breast was a gold star with a Polish white eagle, "*AR*" cipher and crown on a red background. Staff officers had double braid around the sleeve holes.
SASH: Silver-crimson sash tied on the right side.
EQUIPMENT: Red leather belt edged in gold.

Interim uniform

HEADWEAR: Tricorn with golden braid, button and white cockade

STOCK: Black stock.

COAT: Red coat with *bleumourant* collar, cuffs and turnbacks. The coat breast and cuffs had gold buttonhole lace on the left side only. Eight gold buttons on right hand side of coat.

DISTINCTIONS: NCOs had Cuffs were edged in gold lace. Gold buttons.

WAISTCOAT: *Paille Kollet* edged in *bleumourant* lace with two yellow stripes passed through.

BUTTONS: Brass.

LEGWEAR: *Paille* breeches and long black cavalry boots.

EQUIPMENT: White leather belts.

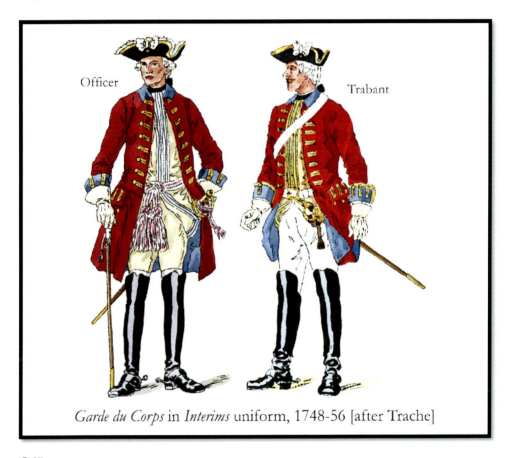

Garde du Corps in *Interims* uniform, 1748-56 [after Trache]

Officer

HEADWEAR: Black tricorn with gold edging and white feathers.

COAT: Long red coat lined with *bleumourant*. The *Bleumourant* collar, cuffs and turnbacks. The coat breast and cuffs had gold buttonhole lace. Eight gold buttons on right hand side of coat.

BUTTONS: Gold.

WAISTCOAT: *Paille Kollet* edged in golden lace with two *bleumourant* stripes passed through.

SASH: Silver-crimson sash tied on the right hand side.

Trabant of the Garde du Corps in Exercier Kollet 1745-1810

Exercise uniform.

STOCK: Red

COAT: White coat with *bleumourant* turnbacks, cuffs and lapels. However, Brauer shows the coat to be red.

BUTTONS: Brass.

DISTINCTIONS: NCOs had gold lace around cuffs and turnbacks.

STABLE CLOTHES: Sail cloth stable smocks and red camp caps with *bleumourant* forehead edge.

HORSE FURNITURE: Officers had *bleumourant* saddlecloths and pistol holsters with golden lace. NCOs and men had yellow edgings and the Saxon Coat of Arms with crown.

Trumpeters and Kettledrummers

These wore the court livery.

COAT: Lemon yellow coat with *bleumourant* collar, cuffs and lapels. The silver braids with two *bleumourant* velvet stripes passed through.

WAISTCOAT: *Bleumourant* waistcoat,

BUTTONS: Silver

LEGWEAR: *Paille* breeches.

EQUIPMENT: Kettledrums were silver with *bleumourant* silver hangings. Trumpets for parade were silver with bleumourant-silver strings and tassels. On service brass trumpets were used with bleumourant-white banner.

HORSE FURNITURE: *Bleumourant* saddlecloth and pistol holders with white edgings with two bleumourant stripes passed through.

Trumpeter of the *Garde du Corps*, 1740-56 [Trache]

Campaign History

Fought in Pomerania (1733), Poland (1733-35) then during the War of Austrian Succession in Bohemia and Saxony (1741-42 and 1744-45) Seven Years War: At the end of August 1756, the regiment retired to Pirna with the rest of the Saxon army and was deployed on the right wing under von Arnim, as part of von Rechenberg Brigade. Taken prisoner at the Lilienstein near Pirna on 15 October 1756 and the men were forcibly drafted to the Prussian Garde du Corps. Most absconded from Prussian service and these were collected in Hungary into grenadier companies. In 1761 there were formed into the *Reiter* Regiment [also known as the Schleiben Cuirassier Regiment.]

Karabinier-Garde Regiment

Raised as a Dragoon Regiment von Feilitzsch in April 1713 by Margrave von Anspach-Bayreuth when it entered Saxon service. In 1715, it became Saxon Dragoon Regiment Flemming. In 1717, it absorbed men from the disbanded Königin Cuirassier Regiment and was renamed Baudissin-Karabinier Regiment. In 1729 it was entitled Karabinier-Garde Regiment and was enhanced by drafts from the other cavalry and was stationed in Warsaw to do palace guard duty. In 1749, it was reduced by four companies. In 1764 it was renamed Karabinier-Regiment.

Inhaber
Dragoons
1717 *Flemming*
Carabinier
1718 *Baudissin*
Karabinier-Garde
1730 *Karabinier-Garde* (GM. von Rex)
Karabinier
1764 Brühl
1786 *Bassewitz*
1791 *Liebenau*
1792 *Zezschwitz*
1810 Disbanded

Karabinier-Garde Regiment

Commander
c1756 *GM. von Zezschwitz* (1758 GL)

Uniform 1735-45
HEADWEAR: Black tricorn with gold trim and white rosette on left side.

STOCK: White changed to red in 1740.

COAT: White coat line red with red collar, cuffs and lapels. The turnbacks were fastened with a button.

KAMISOL: White collarless long-sleeved waistcoat with horizontal pockets with 3 buttons with scarlet turnbacks edged yellow.

LEDERKOLLER: Buff collarless leather coat had horizontal pockets with three buttons and fastened with hooks instead of buttons.

BUTTONS: Brass.

CUIRASS: Two blackened plates without fittings edged in red worn over the waistcoat or *Lederkoller* and under the coat.

LEGWEAR: Leather breeches and black leather boots.

EQUIPMENT: Buff leather belts. Cartridge box belt was worn over left shoulder. Broadsword scabbards were worn on the belt over right shoulder.

Musician (1738-44)

HEADWEAR: Black tricorn with gold trim and white rosette.
STOCK: White.
COAT: Yellow coat with light blue collar, cuffs and turnbacks. White lace on lapels.
WAISTCOAT: Light blue collarless long-sleeved waistcoat.

Trumpeter of the Carabinier-Garde, 1738-1744 [after Trache]

Uniform (1745-61)

HEADWEAR: Black tricorn with gilded lace and button. White bow cockade.
STOCK: Red.
COAT: White coat with scarlet collar, cuffs, lapels and turnbacks.
 KOLLET: *Paille Kollet* with turnbacks edged red-black-yellow-red-yellow-black-red.
WAISTCOAT: Scarlet with golden tresses was not always worn. Normally the *Kollet* was worn instead.

Saxon Army 1740-1763

BUTTONS: Brass.

CLOAK: Scarlet cloak with white collar.

LEGWEAR: Light straw [light *paille*] breeches.

EQUIPMENT: All leather white.

HORSE-FURNITURE: Troopers had red saddlecloths edged yellow in which two red stripes, the king's ciphers and crown in yellow. Officers had red saddlecloths with gold lace, king's ciphers and crown.

DISTINCTIONS: Corporal had gold lace on the cuffs but none on their lapels or turnbacks. Officers had broad gold laces on their *Kollet*.

Trumpeter/Kettledrummer

COATS: Red coat with white collar, cuffs and turnbacks. Gold lace with two red velvet stripes passed through. . On each side of the coat front 6 laces (yellow with two red stripes) placed in 1-2-3.

BUTTONS: brass buttons.

EQUIPMENT: Trumpets silver for parade, otherwise brass with red-gold cords. The regiment carried the captured silver kettledrums that were captured from Prussian Dragoon Regiment von Röell or Holstein on 13 December 1745. The drum banners were possibly red with golden embroideries.

Carabinier-Garde, 1748 [after Trache]

Campaign History

Served in Poland and Pomerania (1713-17) and Poland (1733-35).

War of Austrian Succession: It served in Bohemia, Silesia and Saxony (1740-42 and 1744-45).

Seven Years War. Stationed in Poland so missed the capitulation of the most of the Saxon Army. In 1757, the regiment served with the Austrian army until the end of the war. The regiment with 2 squadrons (350 men) fought at Kolin (18 June 1757) as part of *Köbel Brigade* in the Corps of *Graf Colloredo* and was not engaged at Moys (7 Sept) in Althann Cavalry Brigade.

Cadets

The Notable Company of Cadets was raised in 1692 and disbanded in 1756 when some of the cadets were distributed among the Prussian infantry regiments. It was re-raised in 1763.

Cadet, 1750 [after Trache]

HEADWEAR: Black tricorn with silver lace and button. White cockade, silver-crimson pompom.

COAT: Red coat with white collar, lapels, cuffs and turnbacks.

BUTTONS: Silver buttons and buttonhole lace arranged 2:2:2:2 on lapels.

GLOVES: White.

LEGWEAR: White breeches, white gaiters with brass buttons and black leather shoes.

EQUIPMENT: Black leather cartridge box with silver cipher. Sword in brown leather with silver metalwork, grip and hilt.

DISTINCTIONS: As above with silver lace on the buttonholes. Staff officers had silver-crimson sword knot.

Fahne of the Saxon Cadet Corps, c1747

Flag of the Cadet Corps (1747-1865)
[Hotthenroth (1910)]

Chapter 4:
Saxon Infantry (1735-63)

During the War of Polish Succession there were nine infantry regiments consisting of a regimental staff and twelve companies in two battalions, totalling 1,463 men.[32]

OOB 10: Saxon infantry regiments during the War of Polish Succession.

Nine Infantry Regiments
I-II/IR1 *Leib-regiment*
I-II/IR2 *von Haxthausen*
I-II/IR3 *du Caila,*
I-II/IR4 *Sachsen-Weissenfels*
I-II/IR5 *Sachsen-Gotha*
I-II/IR6 *von Wilcke*
I-II/IR7 *von Löwendal*
I-II/IR7 *Sachsen-Weimar*
I-II/IR10 *von Unruh*

Freikorps
Grenadier Battalion Graf Friesen (6 coys)
Grenadier-Frei Kompagnie Königlich Prinz
Grenadier-Frei Kompagnie Scharzburg-Rudolstadt
Grenadier-Frei Kompagnie Sorau-Promnitz

On 1 July 1732, the infantry regiments were reorganised into eight companies with a total 1,441 men.[33]

Regimental staff (21 men):
1 *Oberst*, 1 *Oberst-lieutenant*, 2 major, 1 *Regiments-Quartiermeister*, 1 adjutant, 1 *Stabs-Feldscher*, 1 *Geistlicher* and 13 others.

Company (12 companies of 120 men):
1 *Kapitän*, 1 *Premierleutnant*, 2 *Sous-Leutnante*, 2 Sergeants, 1 *Gefreiten-Korporal*, 1 *Fourier*, 1 *Feldscher*, 5 corporals (including one grenadier corporal), 4 *Gefreiter*, 2 drummers, 1 *Zimmermann*, 11 grenadiers, 88

During the Austrian War of Succession, Saxony mobilised twelve infantry regiments and a Fusilier Regiment. Each infantry battalion now had two 3-pdr *Geschwindstück* Regimental Guns. [See p178-181]

---

[32] Müller (1984) 34
[33] Müller (1984) 34

In 1748, the infantry was reduced by 44 musketeer companies and four infantry regiments [2. Garde IR, IR10 von Jasmund, IR11 von Allnpeck and IR12 Bellegarde] were disbanded with the men being distributed as shown in OOB 11. The grenadier companies of the four disbanded infantry regiments were formed into the Bellegarde Grenadier Battalion. Each infantry regiment was reorganised into two grenadier and twelve musketeer companies split between two battalions.[34]

Surgeon and auditor, 1753 [after Trache]

---

[34] Hasse & Eichhorn (1936) 12

OOB 11: Distribution of disbanded infantry regiments in 1748.[35]

    2nd Garde IR was disbanded (
        3 coys to IR1 *Königin*
        4 coys to IR4 *Prinz Clemens*
        4 coys to IR8 *Graf Brühl*
    IR10 von Jasmund was disbanded
        3 coys to Fus Regt *von Rochow*
        4 coys to IR9 *Graf Stollberg*
        4 coys to IR5 *Graf Friese*
    IR11 von Allnpeck was disbanded
        4 coys to *Garde zu Fuss*
        4 coys to IR2 *Prinz Gotha*
        3 coys to IR7 *Prinz Xaver*
    IR12 Graf Bellegarde was disbanded
        1 coy to IR1 *Königin*
        4 coys to IR3 *von Frankenberg*
        4 coys to IR5 *von Minckwitz*
        1 coy to IR7 *Prinz Xaver*
        1 coy to Fus Bn *Rochow*

According to the 1753 Saxon Drill Regulations, each regiment of about 1,160 men formed two battalions with ten companies of musketeers and 2 companies of grenadiers. Each musketeer company had 95 men, each grenadier company had 97 grenadiers and there were 17 men in the regimental staff. The exceptions were the Kurprinzessin-Grenadier-Battalion of 5 companies (539 grenadiers) and the Leib-Grenadier-Garde Regiment of 14 grenadier companies formed into 2 battalions (1,684 men).

The new 1753 Saxon Drill Regulations were based upon the Prussian drill with some Austrian drill elements. The infantry battalion was formed 3 deep and divided into four divisions, eight half-divisions or sixteen *Pelotons* (Platoons). In attack, it was expected to maintain a slow and continual advance until 250 to 200 paces when "rolling" fire by the sub-divisions was employed. At 100 paces, the infantry would advance at a faster pace interrupted by three halts for delivering a general battalion volley by the second and third rank until 20 paces. If the enemy held their ground, the first rank would now fire followed by the entire battalion

IR5 Minkwitz, 1756

[35] Hasse & Eichhorn (1936) 12

charging home with the bayonet. If charged by cavalry, the battalion was to hold its fire until the horse approached to 10 paces.

Infantry Staff
  1 *Oberst*, 1 *Oberst-Leutnant*, 2 *Majore*, 1 *Regiments-Quartiermeister*,
  2 *Adjutanten*, 6 *Hoboisten*, 1 *Regiments-Tambour*, 1 *Profos*, 1 *Knecht*,
  plus 1 *Wagenmeister* and the corresponding number of *Knechte* [drivers].

Grenadier Company:
  1 *Kapitän*, 1 *Premierleutnant*, 2 *Sous-leutnante*, 3 *Sergeanten*, 1 *Fourier*,
  1 *Feldscher*, 5 *Korporale*, 2 *Pfeifer*, 3 *Tamboure*, 2 *Zimmerleute*, 76 *Grenadiere*.

Musketeer company:
  1 *Kapitän*, 1 *Premierleutnant*, *Sous-Leutnant*, 1 *Fähnrich*, 3 *Sergeanten*,
  1 *Gefreiten-Korporal*, 1 *Fourier*, 1 *Feldscher*, 5 *Korporale*, 3 *Tamboure*,
  1 *Zimmermann*, 76 men.

In 1756, the grenadier companies were formed into seven elite grenadier battalions. [See OOB 13] Each infantry regiment accounted for 29 wagons and 140 horses.

OOB 12: The Saxon Auxiliary Corps of Prinz Xaver in 11 March 1758.

	Grenadier Coy
I/*Garde zu Fuss*	1 coy
I-II/IR *Kurprinzessin*	2 coys
I/IR1 *Prinz Joseph*	1 coy *Leib Grenadier Garde*
I/IR2 *Prinz Sachsen-Gotha*	1 coy from gunners (until 1758)
I-II/IR3 *Friedrich August*	2 coys
I/IR4 *Prinz Clemens*	1 coy from *Garde du Corps* (until 1760)
I/IR5 *von Minckwitz*	1 coy of cavalrymen (until 1760)
I/IR6 *Prinz Maximilian*	1 coy *Leib Grenadier Garde* (until 1761)
I-II/IR7 *Xaver*	2 coys
I/IR8 *Brühl*	1 coy from *Garde du Corps* (until 1760)
I/IR9 *Lubomirski*	1 coy from gunners (until July 1758)
I/*Fus Regt von Rochow*	1 coy of cavalrymen

The Saxon Auxiliary Corps marched through southern Germany to assemble in Strasbourg by July 1758. In 1761, all twelve infantry regiments were now re-organised into four musketeer companies (121 men) and one grenadier company (98 men) plus two regimental 4-pdrs supplied by the French from the Strasbourg Arsenal. A cavalry regiment was formed from former troopers. The grenadiers were formed into the Leib-Grenadier-Garde Battalion and two Field-Grenadier-Battalions.[36]

---

[36] Otto Cross (1902)

Saxon Infantry
IR1 Königin

Raised in 1673. In 1748 it was augmented by three companies of the disbanded 2nd Garde IR and one company of IR12 Bellegarde, only to be reduced by six companies the next year. The *Reglement* of 1753 stated that the regiment had ten companies of musketeers and two companies of grenadiers in two battalions. After the capitulation at Pirna in October 1756, the whole regiment refused to swear an oath to the King of Prussia so was disbanded and the men distributed among the Prussian infantry. In 1757 the regiment reformed with a battalion of four companies plus a grenadier company taken from men of the former *Leib-Grenadier-Garde* in Hungary. It fought with the French armies until 1763 when it was reorganised on its return to Saxony into fourteen companies in three battalions. In 1778 the regiment was reduced to ten companies in two battalions.

Inhaber
1673 *Prinz Christian von Sachsen-Weissenfels*
1689 *Herzog Christian August von Sachsen-Zeit*
1692 *von Schöning*
1693 *von Bornstädt / von Bornstedt*
1700 *Kurprinz*
1713 *Königlicher Prinz*
1729 *Kronprinz*
1733 *Leib-regiment*
1737 *Königliche Leib-Garde zu Fuss*[37]
Dec 1740 *Königin*[38]
1756 Disbanded
1757 [New] *Prinz Joseph von Sachsen* [re-raised]
1763 *Kurfürst*
1778 *Anhalt*
1783 *Brühl*
1786 *Hartitzsch*
1794 *Wiedemann*
1795 *Niesemeuschel*
1810 Vacant
1813 Disbanded

Commander
1739 *Oberst von Münchau*[39]
1759 *Oberst-Lt von Geysau*[40]
1763 *Oberst Frhr. von Rohr*

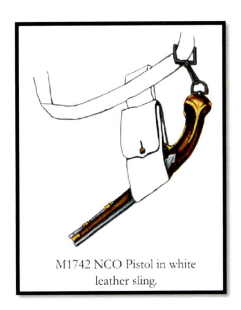

M1742 NCO Pistol in white leather sling.

---

[37] When combined with Leib-Grenadier-Garde.
[38] Separated from *Leib-Grenadier-Garde*. The Chef was Maria Josepha, *Kurfürstin* of Saxony, Queen of Poland.
[39] Died as LG in 1759.
[40] *Oberst* in 1759

Saxon Army 1740-1763

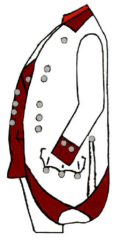

IR1 Königin, 1742-52

Uniform (1742-52)
HEADWEAR: Black tricorn laced white with white-red pompons.
STOCK: Red.
COAT: White coat without lapels and no shoulder straps.
BUTTONS: Brass with yellow buttonhole lace.
COLLAR and CUFFS: Scarlet.
TURNBACKS: Scarlet.
WAISTCOAT: Scarlet.

IR1 Königin, 1753-60

Uniform (1753-60)
HEADWEAR: Black tricorn laced white with white-red pompons.
STOCK: Red.
COAT: White coat without lapels and no shoulder straps.
BUTTONS: Brass.
COLLAR and CUFFS: Deep red.
TURNBACKS: Deep red.
WAISTCOAT: Deep red.

IR1 Prinz Joseph, 1761-63

Uniform (1761-70)
HEADWEAR: Musketeers wore the black tricorn with white lace.
STOCK: Red.
COAT: White with deep red lapels.
BUTTONS: White metal buttons arranged 2:2:2:2.
COLLAR: Deep red.
CUFFS: Deep red with two vertical buttons.
TURNBACKS: Deep red.
WAISTCOAT: **Deep red** changed to white in 1771.

Campaign History

It participated in the campaigns against the French 1673-77. In 1683, it was with the army at the relief of Vienna. It was in Hungary 1686-88, on the Rhine 1688-95, Hungary 1696 and then Poland 1697-99.

War of the Spanish Succession: The regiment served with the Imperial army under Prince Eugene. In 1705, it returned to Saxony. In 1706, it was in Poland. From 1707-12, it took part in the campaigns in Flanders. It then served in Poland once more until 1717.

War of the Polish Succession: It fought in Poland in 1734-35.

War of the Austrian Succession: It served in Bohemia, Moravia and Saxony in 1741-42, and 1744-45.

Seven Years War: It was part of von Stollberg Brigade at Pirna and disbanded. The regiment refused to swear allegiance to Frederick II so the men were distributed among the Prussian infantry units. In 1757, a new regiment was raised named Prinz Joseph which served with the French Army until 1763. Fought at Lutterberg (10 Oct 1758) where its determined attacks were instrumental in the victory, at Bergen (13 Apr 1759) and Minden (1 Aug 1759.)

Musketeer of IR1 Königin in Waistcoat 1761-1781 [Wilhelm Dietrich, 1914]

IR2 Sachsen-Gotha

Formed in 1682 and took part the next year in the relief of Vienna. In 1748, it was augmented by four coys from the disbanded IR Allnpeck. In 1749, six coys were disbanded. On 15 October 1756, the regiment was captured at Pirna and forced into Prussian service as *S54 von Saldern*. In 1757, it was reformed as a single battalion regiment of 4 coys and grenadier coy raised from former artillerymen. It returned to Saxony in 1763 when it was reorganised into 3 Bns in 14 coys. In 1778 the regiment was reduced to 2 Bns in 10 coys.

Inhaber
1682 *Kuffer*
1689 *Uetterodt*
1697 *Holstein*
1699 *Königin*
1727 *Prinz Joseph*
1728 *Rutowski*
1729 *Böhnen*
1730 *Haxthausen*
1741 *Frankenberg*
1744 *Johann Adolf von Sachsen-Gotha-Altenburg* [Disbanded 1756]
1756-63 Prussian S54[41]
1758 [New] *Johann Adolf von Sachsen-Gotha-Altenburg*[42]
1799 *Low*
1813 Disbanded

IR2 von Haxthausen (1734-41)
IR2 Frankenburg (1741-42)

Commanders
1744 *Oberst von Ütterodt*.
1757 *Oberst von Lecoq*.
1763 *Oberst von Uetterrodt* [d. as GM in 1781]

Uniform (1734-42)
HEADWEAR: Black tricorn with white lace and white cockade.
STOCK: Red.
COAT: White.
BUTTONS: White metal.
FACINGS: Brown.
WAISTCOAT: Brown.
LEGWEAR: White breeches, black gaiters and shoes.

---

[41] Oct 1756 *W. von Saldern*, 8 Dec 1758-1763 *F.E.F. von Plotho* [Bleckwenn (1987) IV: 73]
[42] In 1758, the reformed single battalion regiment had four musketeer companies and a grenadier company from former gunners that was disbanded in August 1758 to reform two artillery companies.

Saxon Army 1740-1763

IR2 von Haxthausen, 1734-41 [after Trache]

Saxon Army 1740-1763

IR2 von Frankenburg
1742-44

IR2 Sachsen-Gotha
1745-60

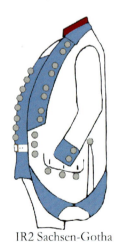

IR2 Sachsen-Gotha
1761-70

Uniform (1742-44)
HEADWEAR: Black tricorn laced white with white and yellow pompons.
STOCK: Red.
COAT: White coat without lapels and shoulder straps.
BUTTONS: White metal.
FACINGS: Sky blue.
WAISTCOAT: Sky blue.
LEGWEAR: Sky blue breeches until 1745.

Uniform (1753-60)
HEADWEAR: Black tricorn laced white with white and yellow pompons.
STOCK: Red.
COAT: White coat without lapels.
BUTTONS: White metal.
FACINGS: Sky blue.
WAISTCOAT: Sky blue.

Uniform (1761-70)
HEADWEAR: As above.
STOCK: Red.
COAT: White with Sky blue lapels and no shoulder straps.
BUTTONS: White metal buttons arranged 2:2:2:2.
COLLAR and CUFFS: Sky blue.
TURNBACKS: Sky blue.
WAISTCOAT: Sky blue.

Campaign History
War of the Polish Succession: Served in Poland (1734-35) and Hungary (1737-39).

War of the Austrian Succession, In Bohemia, Moravia, Silesia and Saxony (1741-45).

Seven Years War: In 1756, the regiment was part of von Risckwitz's Brigade and surrendered at Pirna (15 Oct). Re-raised in 1757 as a single battalion regiment. Fought at Lutterberg (10 Oct), Minden (13 Apr 1759) and Warburg (1760).

IR3 Prinz Friedrich August

The regiment was raised in 1701 by Graf Beichlingen. In 1705-06, it was augmented by incorporating a battalion of French and another from the Dresden garrison. In 1748, it absorbed four companies from the disbanded IR12 Bellegarde and these were disbanded in 1749. In 1758, the regiment retained its grenadiers. In 1763, it became three battalions (14 companies). In 1778, this was reduced to two battalions (10 companies).

Inhaber
1701 *Graf Beichlingen*
1703 *Graf Wackerbarth*
1714 *Graf Friese*
1717 *von Pflugk*
1728 *du Caila*
1740 *Niesemeuschel*
1746 *Frankenberg*
1751 *Prinz Friedrich August of Saxony* [Disbanded Oct 1756]
1756-63 Prussian S56[43]
1757 (New) *Prinz Friedrich August of Saxony*
1764-1815 *Prinz Maximilian of Saxony*

Commander
1752: *GM* Nicolaus *von Pirch*
1757-64: *Oberst von Borck*

IR3 du Caila (1734-40)
IR3 Niesemeuschel (1740-42)

Uniform (1734-45)
HEADWEAR: Black tricorn laced white with white and yellow pompons. Grenadiers wore Prussian style mitre with brass front-plate and headband, yellow back with white piping, white and yellow pom-pom.

COAT: White coat and no shoulder straps.

LAPELS: Yellow with six brass buttons (2:2:2).

FACINGS: Yellow.

BUTTONS: Brass buttons arranged 2:2:2 and three below.

LEGWEAR: Yellow breeches, black gaiters and black shoes. Officers wore yellow breeches.

---

[43] Oct 1756 *J.B. von Loen*, 22 Jan 1758 *S.A. von Kalckreuth*, 9 Dec 1758 *L.F.L. von Wintersheim*, 25 Feb 1759-1763 *F.M. von Horn*. [Bleckwenn (1987) IV: 72]

IR3 von Frankenberg, 1746-51

IR3 Friedrich August, 1753-60

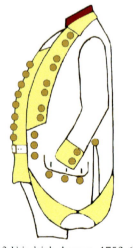

IR3 Friedrich August, 1753-60

Uniform (1746-52)

HEADWEAR: As above

COAT: White coat without lapels and shoulder straps.

FACINGS: Yellow.

BUTTONS: Brass buttons arranged 2:2:2.

LEGWEAR: Yellow breeches were worn until 1745 when they became white breeches. Black gaiters. Officers wore yellow breeches.

Uniform (1753-60)

HEADWEAR: Black tricorn laced white with white and yellow pompons. Until 1756, grenadiers wore Prussian style mitre with brass front-plate and headband, yellow back with white piping, white and yellow pom-pom. From 1757-60, the grenadiers wore a black tricorn laced white.

STOCK: Red.

COAT: White and no shoulder straps.

CUFFS and TURNBACKS: Yellow.

LAPELS: No lapels.

BUTTONS: Brass buttons arranged 1:2:3.

WAISTCOAT: Yellow.

LEGWEAR: White breeches, black gaiters. Officers wore yellow breeches.

Uniform (1761-65)

HEADWEAR: Black tricorn laced white with white and yellow pompons. Officers and NCOs wore a black tricorn laced gold with a white cockade. Grenadiers wore black Austrian style fur bearskin with a brass plate with the electoral crest; falling from the rear of the bearskin were white woollen cords and tassels, the latter with a yellow inner part.

STOCK: Red.

COAT: White with yellow lapels and no shoulder straps.

COLLAR and CUFFS: Yellow.

TURNBACKS: Yellow.

WAISTCOAT: Yellow.

Campaign History

Until 1717 it participated in the campaigns in Poland, Brabant and Pomerania.

War of the Polish Succession: The regiment served in Poland (1734-35).

War of the Austrian Succession: The regiment took part to the campaigns of 1741-42 and 1744-45 in Bohemia, Moravia and Saxony.

Seven Years War: In 1756, the regiment was part of von Gersdorf Brigade at Pirna where it surrendered (15 Oct). The regiment was then forcefully incorporated into the Prussian S56 von Löhn.

On 28 March 1757, the former I Bn of Prussian S56 absconded from Lübben led by Sergeant Seher. This was followed the next day by the II Bn commanded by Sergeant Richter of the Königin IR from Guben. Both battalions reached Meiseritz in Poland where the two sergeants were immediately promoted to captain. Subsequently, the regiment marched to Hungary to join the other Saxon troops gathering there and received the honour to march to the *Grenadiermarsch*.

In 1757, the reformed regiment consisted of two battalions with eight companies plus one Grenadier Company and entered into the French service. The Saxon Auxiliary Corps marched through southern Germany to join Contade's Army in Westphalia by September 1758. Fought at Lutterberg (10 Oct 1758) where its determined attacks were instrumental in the victory, at Bergen (13 Apr 1759) and Minden (1 Aug 1759.)

Saxon IR Prinz Friedrich August 1758

IR4 Prinz Clemens

Raised in 1704 by Herzog Johann George zu Sachsen-Weissenfels and increased to two battalions the next year. In 1748, augmented by 4 coys from the disbanded 2nd Garde zu Fuss and the next year 6 coys were disbanded. Taken prisoner at Pirna in October 1756 and impressed into Prussian service as S58 von Flemming. In 1757, the regiment reformed as single battalion regiment of 4 coys and a grenadier coy raised from dismounted *Guard du Corps*. In 1763, it was reformed into 3 Bns in 14 coys. In 1778, it was reduced to 2 Bns in 10 coys.

IR4 Sachsen-Weisserfels
1742-46

Inhaber
1704 *Herzog von Sachsen-Weissenfels*
1746 *Prinz Clemens von Polen und Sachsen.*[44]
[Disbanded in 1756]
1756-57 Prussian S58[45]
1758 [New] *Prinz Clemens*
1812 *von Steindel*
1813 Disbanded

Commander
c1750 *Oberst von Kötzschau*[46]
1757 *Oberst-Lt. von Kaltenborn*
1760 *Oberst-Lt. von Brandenstein*
1763 *GL Diede von Fürstenberg*

IR4 Prinz Clemens
1746-53

Uniform (1742-52)
HEADWEAR: Black tricorn laced white with white and yellow pompons.
STOCK: Red.
COAT: White coat without collars, lapels and shoulder straps.
BUTTONS: Brass.
FACINGS: French blue.
LEGWEAR: French Blue breeches until 1745 when replaced by white breeches.

---

[44] Bishop of Augsburg and Ratisbon. In 1768 Prince-Elector and Archbishop of Trier.
[45] Oct 1756-Sept 1757 *E.B. Graf von Flemming.* [Bleckwenn (1987) IV: 72]
[46] In 1756 commanded a detachment that reinforced Königstein Fortress and died in 1759.

Uniform (1753-60)
HEADWEAR: Black tricorn laced white with white and yellow pompons.
STOCK: Red
COAT: White coat without lapels and shoulder straps.
BUTTONS: Brass.
FACINGS: French blue.

IR4 Prinz Clemens, 1753-60

Uniform (1761-65)
HEADWEAR: As above.
STOCK: Red.
COAT: White with French blue lapels and no shoulder straps.
BUTTONS: Brass.
FACINGS: French blue.

Campaign History
War of the Polish Succession: Served in Poland (1734), Rhine (1735) and Hungary (1737-39).

War of the Austrian Succession: The regiment took part to the campaigns of 1741, 1742, 1744 and 1745 in Bohemia, Moravia and Saxony (1741-45).

IR4 Prinz Clemens, 1761-70

Seven Years War: In 1756 part of von Bolberitz's Brigade and surrendered at Pirna (15 Oct.) Forcefully incorporated into the Prussian army as S58 von Flemming Fusiliers. In 1757, about 500 men absconded from the Prussian service and marched through Poland to Hungary where the regiment was re-established. In mid September 1758, the regiment was part of the Saxon contingent commanded by Prince Xaver that joined the French army of the Marquis de Contades in Westphalia. Fought at Lutterberg (10 Oct 1758), Bergen (13 Apr 1759), Minden (1 Aug 1759) and Langenfeld (1761).

IR5 Minckwitz

Raised in 1702 by the Margraf von Anspach. In 1709, the Seckendorff Grenadiers entered Saxon service and became an Infantry Regiment in 1711. In 1748, it was augmented by 4 coys from the disbanded IR12 Bellegarde and the next year 6 coys were disbanded. In 1756, the regiment became prisoner at Pirna and turned over into Prussian service as S53 von Manstein. In 1757, it comprised of a single battalion regiment of four companies and a grenadier company from dismounted troopers of the Saxon cuirassier regiments. The grenadier company was disbanded in 1761 and the men were used to form the new Cuirassier Regiment. In 1763, it was reorganised in 3 Bns in 14 coys. In 1778, the regiment was reduced to 2 Bns in 10 coys.

IR5 Minckwitz, 1748-52 [After Trache]

Inhaber
1709 *Graf Seckendorff*
1717 *Diemar*
1719 *von Marancourt*
1723 *Prinz Wilhelm Ludwig von Schwarzenburg-Rudilfstadt*
1728 *Prinz Wilhelm von Sachsen-Gotha*
1734 *Löwendal / Loewendal*
1736 *Graf Sulkowski / Graf Sulkowsky*
1744 *Nicolaus von Pirch*
1746 *Prince Anton von Minckwitz* [Disbanded 1756]
1756-57 Prussian S53[47]

---

[47] Oct 1756-Sept 1757 *C.H. von Manstein.* [Bleckwenn (1987) IV: 72]

1758 [New] *Prince Anton von Minckwitz*
1759-1815 *Prinz Anton von Sachsen*

Commander
1749-56 *GM von Carlowitz*
1757 *Oberst-Lt von Arnim*
1759 *Oberst Frhr. von Spörcken*
1762 *Oberst Graf Byland*
1763 *Oberst von Nitzschwitz* (d. 1763)

Uniform (1753-60)
HEADWEAR: Black tricorn laced white with white and yellow pompons.
STOCK: Red.
COAT: White coat.
LAPELS: None.
FACINGS: French blue.
BUTTONS: White metal buttons arranged 1:2:3.

IR5 Minkwitz (1753-59)
IR5 Prinz Anton (1760)

Uniform (1753-60)
HEADWEAR: Black tricorn laced white with white and yellow pompons.
STOCK: Red.
COAT: White coat
LAPELS: French blue.
FACINGS: French blue.
BUTTONS: White metal buttons arranged 2:2:2:2.

Campaign History
War of the Polish Succession: The regiment served in Poland (1733-35) and in Hungary (1737-39.)

IR5 Prinz Anton (1761-70)

War of the Austrian Succession: The regiment took part to the campaigns in Bohemia, Moravia and Saxony (1742-45).

Seven Years War: In 1756, the regiment was part of von Bolberitz's Brigade that surrendered at Pirna (15 Oct.) and was pressed into Prussian service as S53 von Manstein. In 1757, a new single battalion of 4 coys and grenadier coy formed from dismounted Saxon cuirassier troopers. Fought at Lutterberg (10 Oct 1758), Bergen (13 Apr 1759), Minden (1 Aug 1759), Wildungen (1760), Cassel (1760), Bolstedt (1761) and Speele (1762).

IR6 Prinz Maximilian

Raised in 1711 from two battalions of the Dresden garrison. In 1748 it was augmented by 4 coys of the disbanded Jasmund regiment. In 1749, 6 companies were disbanded. In 1756, the regiment surrendered at Pirna (15 Oct) and was forced into Prussian service as S59 Prinz Friedrich Wilhelm von Preussen (son of Prince Henri.) In 1757, reformed as single battalion regiment in Hungary. In 1763 on its return to Saxony, it was reformed in 3 Bns in 14 coys. In 1778, it was reduced to 2 Bns in 10 coys.

IR Cosel, 1742-46

Inhaber
1711 *Flemming*
1715 *Graf Wackerbarth*
1717 *von Dressky / von Dretzki*
1729 *von Wilke / von Wilcke*
1739 *Graf Cosel / Graf Kosel*
1746 *MG Graf Friese* [d. 1755]
1755 *Prinz Karl Maximilian von Sachsen*
[Disbanded 1756]
1756-57 Prussian S59[48]
1758 [New] *Prinz Karl Maximilian*[49]
1782 *Zanthier*
1798-1815 *Prinz Friedrich August*

Commander
1755 *Oberst Frhr. von Klingenberg*
1759 *Oberst-Lt von Hesler*
1763 *GL von Klingenberg* [Inspector of Infantry.]

Uniform (1742-52)
HEADWEAR: Black tricorn laced white with white and yellow pompons.
STOCK: Red
COAT: White.
BUTTONS: Brass.
FACINGS: Russian green.
LEGWEAR: Russian green breeches until 1746 when they were replaced by white breeches.

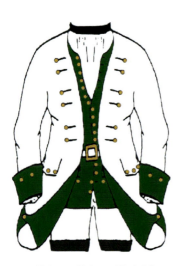

IR6 von Friese, 1746-55

---

[48] Oct 1756-3 Aug 1757 *Friedrich Wilhelm Prinz von Preussen.* [Bleckwenn (1987) IV: 73]
[49] In 1758, the newly raised single battalion regiment had four companies and a grenadier company from the former *Leib-Grenadier-Garde*.

Uniform (1753-60)
HEADWEAR: As above.
STOCK: Red.
COAT: White without shoulder straps and lapels.
BUTTONS: Brass.
FACINGS: Russian green.

Uniform (1761-65)
HEADWEAR: As above.
STOCK: Red.
COAT: White with Russian green lapels and no shoulder straps.
BUTTONS: Brass.
FACINGS: Russian green.

IR6 Maximilian, 1755-60

Campaign History
War of the Polish Succession: The regiment fought in Poland (1733-35.)

War of the Austrian Succession: It served Bohemia, Moravia, Silesia and Saxony (1741-45.)

Seven Years War: In 1756, part of von Stolberg's Brigade that surrendered at Pirna (15 Oct) and forcibly enlisted in the Prussian Army as S59. In 1757, re-raised in Hungary as a single battalion regiment. Fought at Lutterberg (10 Oct 1758), Berger (13 Apr 1759), Minden (1 Aug 1759) and Langensalza (1759).

IR6 Maximilian, 1755-60

IR7 Prinz Xaver

Raised in 1723 as a one battalion regiment to garrison the royal residences. In 1730, it became the Grenadier Regiment Sachsen-Weimar with the addition of a Grenadier Bn from the Duke of Saxe-Weimar and the *Frei-Kompagnie Grenadiers* of the Prinz von Schwarzburg-Rudolfstadt. In 1733, the Duke of Saxe-Weimar recalled his battalion and it was replaced by drafts from the other infantry regiments filled out by new recruits. In 1748, it was augmented with companies from the disbanded IR11 Allnpeck (3 coys) and IR12 Bellegarde (1 coy). In 1749, six companies were disbanded. The Reglement of 1753, stated that the regiment had 2 Bns in 10 companies and 2 grenadier companies.

In October 1756, after the capitulation at Pirna the regiment was impressed into Prussian service as S59 von Bevern Regiment. On 30 March, I Bn absconded and was reformed with 2 Bns of 8 companies plus a grenadier company in Hungary and had the honour to play the Grenadiermarsch. In 1763, it was reformed in 3 Bns of 14 companies. In 1778, the regiment was reduced to 2 Bns of 10 companies.

Inhaber
1723 *Graf Flemming*,
1729 *Graf Wackerbarth*,
1730 *Erbprinz Johann W. von Sachsen-Weimar*
1733 *Prinz Xaver of Poland and Saxony*.[50]
[Disbanded 1756]
1756 Prussian S57[51]
1758 [New] *Prinz Xaver*
1806 *von Oebschelwitz*
1810 Disbanded

Commander
1742 *Oberst von Gersdorff*
1757 *Oberst von Kavanagk* (d. 1761)
1761-68 *Oberst von Carlsburg*

Uniform (1735-48)
HEADWEAR: Black tricorn laced white with white and yellow pompons.
STOCK: Red
BUTTONS: Brass.
COLLAR & CUFFS: Sky blue [*bleumourant*]
TURNBACKS: Sky blue [*bleumourant*]
LAPELS: None
LEGWEAR: Light blue breeches until 1745 and then white. Black gaiters and black shoes.

Uniform (1753-60)
HEADWEAR: Black tricorn laced white with white and yellow pompons.
STOCK: Red
COLLAR and CUFFS: Sky blue [*bleumourant*]
TURNBACKS: Sky blue [*bleumourant*]
LAPELS: None
BUTTONS: Brass.
LEGWEAR: White breeches, black gaiters and black shoes.

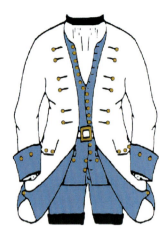
IR7 Xaver, 1742-45

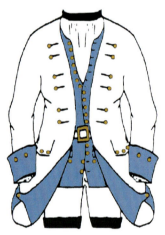
IR7 Xaver, 1746-52

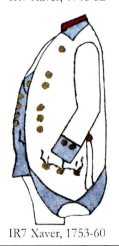
IR7 Xaver, 1753-60

---

[50] LG in 1758.
[51] 1756-Sept 1757 *Prinz Carl von Braunschweig-Bevern (Jung-Bevern)* [Bleckwenn (1987) IV: 72]

Uniform (1761-65)
HEADWEAR: As above.
STOCK: Red.
COLLAR and CUFFS: Sky blue [*bleumourant*]
TURNBACKS: Sky blue [*bleumourant*]
LAPELS: Sky blue [*bleumourant*].
WAISTCOAT: Sky blue [*bleumourant*].
BUTTONS: Brass.
LEGWEAR: White breeches, black gaiters and black shoes.

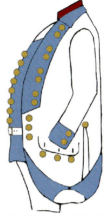

IR7 Xaver, 1761-70

Campaign History
War of Polish Succession: The regiment served in Poland from 1733-36.

War of the Austrian Succession: It took part to the campaigns of 1741-42 and 1744-45 in Bohemia, Moravia, Silesia and Saxony.

Seven Years War: Part of von Gersdorf Brigade at Pirna and after the capitulation became part of the Prussian S57 Jung-Braunschweig. On 30 March 1757, the I Bn absconded from the Prussian service with its flags, regimental guns and pay chest from Crossen under the command of Musketeer Belling of Major Weissenbach's company. Musketeer Belling was reported missing after the passage of the Oder. The battalion finally reached Poland under the command of Sergeant Knabe who was immediately promoted captain. A new regiment was then formed from these troops and included into the Saxon Auxiliary contingent serving with the French until 1763. Fought at Minden (1759) and Warburg (1760).

IR7 Prinz Xaver, 1756

IR8 Graf Brühl
Raised in 1741 from contingents from the other infantry regiments. In 1748 it was received 4 coys of the disbanded 2nd Garde zu Fuss and the next year 6 coys were disbanded. In 1756, surrendered at Pirna and forcibly became S51 von Wylich. In 1758, the newly raised single battalion regiment of 4 coys and a grenadier company from men of the dismounted Garde du Corps. In 1761, the grenadier company was used to form the new Cuirassier Regiment. In 1763, reformed in 3 Bns in 14 coys. In 1778, the regiment was reduced to 2 battalions in 10 coys.

Saxon Army 1740-1763

Inhaber
1741 *Heinrich Graf von Brühl*[52] [Disbanded 1756]
1756 Prussian S51[53]
1758 *Graf Heinrich von Brühl*
1764 *Borcke / Borke*
1775 *Karlsburg*
1786 *Langenau*
1794 *Winckel / Winkel*
1798 *Sänger*
1808 *von Cerrini* [Disbanded 1810]

Commander
1741 *Oberst von Bolbritz*
1752 *Oberst von der Brüggen*
1757 *Oberst-Lt von Thiele*
1758 *Oberst von der Brüggen*
1760 *Oberst Karl von Brühl*

IR8 Graf Brühl, 1741-60

Uniform (1734-52)
HEADWEAR: Black tricorn laced white with white and yellow pompons.
STOCK: Red
COLLAR and CUFFS: Red.
TURNBACKS: Red.
WAISTCOAT: Red.
BUTTONS: Brass

Uniform (1753-70)
HEADWEAR: As above.
STOCK: Red.
COLLAR and CUFFS: Red.
TURNBACKS: Red.
WAISTCOAT: Red.
BUTTONS: Brass.

IR8 Graf Brühl, 1753-65

Campaign History
Seven Years War: In 1756, it was as part of von Risckwitz's Brigade and surrendered at Pirna (15 Oct) and forcibly incorporated into the Prussian Army as S51 von Wylich. In 1757, re-raised in Hungary. Fought at Lutterberg (10 Oct), Bergen (13 Apr 1759), Minden (1 Aug 1759) and Warburg (1760).

---

[52] **Graf Heinrich von Brühl** (1700-1763) who became Prime Minister of Saxony in 1746.
[53] Oct 1756-31 July 1757 *F. von Wylich* [Bleckwenn (1987) IV: 72]

IR9 Fürst Lubomirski

Raised in 1742. In 1748, it was received 4 coys from the disbanded IR10 Jasmund and the next year 6 coys were disbanded. In 1756, the regiment surrendered at Pirna and pressed into Prussian service as S55 von Hauss. In 1757, the re-raised single battalion regiment of 4 companies and a grenadier company from former gunners was formed in Hungary. In 1763, reformed into 3 Bns in 14 coys. In 1778, the regiment was reduced to 2 Bns in 10 coys.

Officer of IR9 Graf Stollberg, 1742-52 [after Trache]

Inhaber

1742 *Graf Stollberg-Rossla*
1752 *GM Fürst Lubomirski / Fürst Lubomirsky* [Disbanded 1756]
1756-63 Prussian S55[54]
1757 [New] *GM Fürst Lubomirski*[55]

---

[54] Oct 1756 *F.C. von Hauss*, 25 Dec 1760-1763 *L.P. Röbel* [Bleckwenn (1987) IV: 72]

1763 *Block*
1778 *Lecoq*
1789 *Boblick*
1792 *Bomsdorff*
1794 *Nostitz*
1802 *Thümmel*
1800 *von Burgsdorff*
1810 Disbanded

Commander
1752 *Oberst von Bomsdorff*
1757 *Oberst-Lt von Römer*
1759 *Oberst von Thiele*
1764 *Oberst von Zanthier*

IR9 Lubomirski, 1753-60

Uniform (1753-60)
HEADWEAR: Black tricorn laced white with white and yellow pompons.
STOCK: Red
BUTTONS: White metal (1:2:3).
COLLAR and CUFFS: Yellow.
TURNBACKS: Yellow.
WAISTCOAT: Yellow.

Uniform (1761-65)
HEADWEAR: As above.
STOCK: Red.
COAT: White with yellow lapels and no shoulder straps.
BUTTONS: White metal.
COLLAR and CUFFS: Yellow.
TURNBACKS: Yellow.
WAISTCOAT: Yellow.

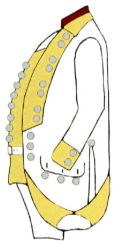

IR9 Lubomirski, 1761-70

Campaign History
Seven Years War: In 1756, it was part of von Bolberitz's Brigade that surrendered at Pirna (15 Oct) and forcibly enlisted into the Prussian Army as S50 Hauss Fusiliers. In 1757, re-raised in Hungary. Fought at Lutterberg (10 Oct 1758), Bergen (13 Apr 1759), Minden (1 Aug 1759) and Warburg (1760).

---

[55] Became *Chef* of the *Leib-Grenadier-Garde* in 1765.

Fusilier Regiment Rochow

Fusiliers Regiment Rochow 1745-50

Formed in 1741. In 1748, it received 3 coys of the disbanded IR10 Jasmund and 1 coy of IR12 Bellegarde. In 1749, 6 coys were disbanded. In 1756, the regiment surrendered at Pirna and pressed into Prussian service as S50 von Wietersheim.

Inhaber
Fusilier Regiment
1741 *Oberst von Schönberg* [killed at Striegau]
1745 *GdI von Rochow*[56] [Disbanded Oct 1756]
1756 Prussian S50[57]
1758 [New] *Rochow*[58]
Infantry Regiment
1762 *Prinz Maximilian von Sachsen*
1764 *GL von Klingenberg*
1779 *Riedesel*
1786 *Lindt*
1801 *Rechten*
1810 Disbanded

Commander
1746 *Oberst Diede von Fürstenberg.*
1757 *Oberst von Bennigsen.*
1762 *GL Graf Entremont Bellegarde.*
1763 *Oberst von Reitzenstein*

Fusilier Uniform (1742-52)
HEADWEAR: Brass fusilier cap or tricorn.
STOCK: Red
COAT: Green coat without collar, lapels and shoulder straps.
CUFFS: Red
WAISTCOAT: Red
BUTTONS: Brass.

Fus Regt Schönburg (1742-45)
Fus Regt Rocow (1745-60)

---
[56] Died in Vienna in 1759
[57] Oct 1756-30 July 1757 *L.F.L. von Wietersheim* [Bleckwenn (1987) IV: 72]
[58] In 1758, the single battalion regiment of 4 companies had a grenadier company from dismounted troopers of the Saxon cuirassier regiments. In 1761, the grenadier company was disbanded and the men formed the new Cuirassier Regiment.

Saxon Army 1740-1763

Fusilier Uniform (1752-62)
HEADWEAR: Brass fusilier cap or tricorn.
STOCK: Red
COAT: Green coat without lapels and shoulder straps.
COLLAR and CUFFS: Red
WAISTCOAT: Red
BUTTONS: Brass.

Campaign History
War of the Austrian Succession: It participated in the campaigns in Bohemia, Moravia, Silesia and Saxony until 1745.

Seven Years War: In 1756, part of von Risckwitz's Brigade that surrendered at Pirna (15 Oct). Re-raised in 1757 as a single Bn. Fought at Lutterberg (10 Oct 1758), Bergen (13 Apr 1759), Minden (1 Aug 1759) and Warburg (1760).

Fusilier Regiment von Rochow, 1753-61

Disbanded Infantry Regiments in 1748
IR10 Römer (1680-48)

Formed in 1680

Inhaber
1680 *von Loeben*
1686 *Zinzendorff*
1692 *von Rubel / von Roebel*
1700 *von Steinau*
1701 *Fürst Furstenberg*
1716 *von Browne*
1717 *Marche*
1732 *von Diessbach*
1733 *von Unruh*
1742 *Römer*
1744 *Franz von Pirch / Jung Pirch*
1746 *von Jasmund*
1748 Disbanded

IR10 Römer (1742-44
IR10 Jung Pirch (1744-46)
IR10 von Jasmund (1746-58)

Uniform (1742-48)
HEADWEAR: Black tricorn laced white.
BUTTONS: White metal (2:2:2).
FACINGS and WAISTCOAT: Grass green

IR11 Allnpeck (1702-48)

IR11 von Allnpeck
1742-48

Formed in 1702.

Inhaber
1702 *Wustromirsky*
1707 *Frhr. von Ogilvy* [d. 1710]
1710 *von der Goltz*
1717 *Seissan (Soissan)*
1717 *Fitzner*
1719 *de la Serre*
1724 *von Löwendal*
1733 *von Rochow*
1739 *von Allnpeck*
1748 Disbanded

Uniform (1742-48)
HEADWEAR: Black tricorn laced white.
BUTTONS: White metal (3:3:3).
FACINGS and WAISTCOAT: Grass green

IR12 Bellegarde (1742-48)

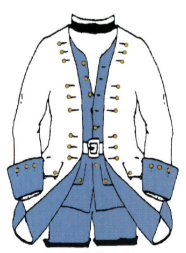

IR12 Bellegarde
1742-48

Formed in 1742

Inhaber
1742 *Graf Bellegarde*
1748 Disbanded

Uniform (1742-48)
HEADWEAR: Black tricorn laced white.
BUTTONS: Brass (3:3:3).
FACINGS and WAISTCOAT: Grass green

Musketeer Uniform
Infantry Uniform (1734-42)
HEADWEAR: Black tricorn laced white with white and yellow pompons. Fatigue cap similar to the French *"pokalem"* was white with facing colour lace around the edge and white tassel at the rear.

STOCK: Red.

COAT: White with 6 buttons on the left side and 3 more on the right side. Horizontal pockets, each with 3 buttons. Collar and cuffs with 3 buttons in facing colour. No shoulder straps. The lapels were in facing colour. The turnbacks in facing colour were fastened with a small button.

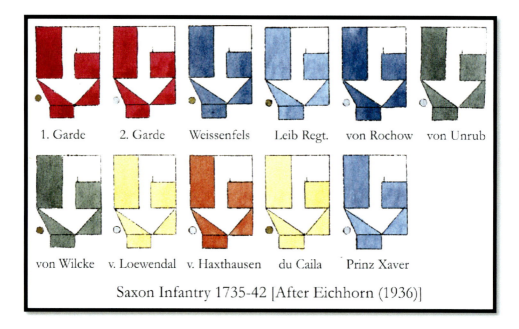

Saxon Infantry 1735-42 [After Eichhorn (1936)]

WAISTCOAT: Waistcoat in facing colour with horizontal pockets and buttons.

LEGWEAR: Breeches were in facing colour until about 1745. Black or white gaiters and black shoes. Grey sailcloth over-trousers for exercises and fatigue wear.

EQUIPMENT: Brown calfskin pack and haversack were carried with the tents in the baggage train. Black cartridge box with brass buckles, metalwork and white shoulder straps.

TENTS: Tents were made of raw linen.

SIDEARMS: Troopers were armed with a musket, a bayonet and a sword. Musket covers were of black polished linen.

Table 2: Uniform of Saxon Infantry Regiments 1734-42.
According to the order of 23 July 1734.[59]

Regiment	Coat	Cuffs, turnbacks	Lapels	Waistcoat	Buttons
IR1 *Kronprinz* (1729) *Leib-Regiment* (1733) *Königin* (1740)	white	sky blue [*bleumourant*]	sky blue [*bleumourant*]	sky blue [*bleumourant*]	brass
IR2 *Haxthausen* (1730) *Frankenberg* (1741)	white	cinnamon brown [*zimtbraun*]	cinnamon brown [*zimtbraun*]	cinnamon brown [*zimtbraun*]	white metal
IR3 *Du Caila* (1728) *Niesemeuschel* (1740)	white	yellow [*gelb*]	yellow [*gelb*]	yellow [*gelb*]	brass
IR4 *Sachsen-Weissenfels* (1704)	white	dark blue [*dunkelblau*]	dark blue [*dunkelblau*]	dark blue [*dunkelblau*]	brass
IR5 *Löwendal* (1734) *Sulkowski* (1737)	white	yellow [*gelb*]	yellow [*gelb*]	yellow [*gelb*]	white metal
IR6 *von Wilke* (1729) *von Kosel* (1739)	white	dark green [*dunkelgrün*]	dark green [*dunkelgrün*]	dark green [*dunkelgrün*]	brass
IR7 *Graf Wackerbarth* (1729) *Sachsen-Weimar* (1730) *Prinz Xaver* (1733)	white	sky blue [*bleumourant*]	sky blue [*bleumourant*]	sky blue [*bleumourant*]	white metal
IR10 *von Unruh* (1733) *Römer* (1742)	white	dark green [*dunkelgrün*]	dark green [*dunkelgrün*]	dark green [*dunkelgrün*]	white metal
IR11 (Est. 1702) *Von Rochow* (1733) *von Allnpeck* (1739)	white	French blue [*dunkelblau*]	French blue [*dunkelblau*]	French blue [*dunkelblau*]	white metal
Raised in 1741					
Fus Regt (Est. 1741) *von Schönberg* (1741)	green	scarlet	scarlet	scarlet	white metal
IR8 *Graf Brühl* (Est. 1741)	white	red	red	red	brass
Freikorps					
Leib Frei-Kompagnie Grenadier [60]	white	sky blue [*bleumourant*]	sky blue [*bleumourant*]	sky blue [*bleumourant*]	white metal
Frei-Kompagnie Sorau Promnitz	white	sky blue [*bleumourant*]	sky blue [*bleumourant*]	sky blue [*bleumourant*]	white metal
Frei-Kompagnie Sulk	*paille*	red	red	red	white metal

---

[59] Friedrich (1998) 16
[60] Also known as Hubertsburger Frei-Kompagnie Grenadiers.

Saxon Army 1740-1763

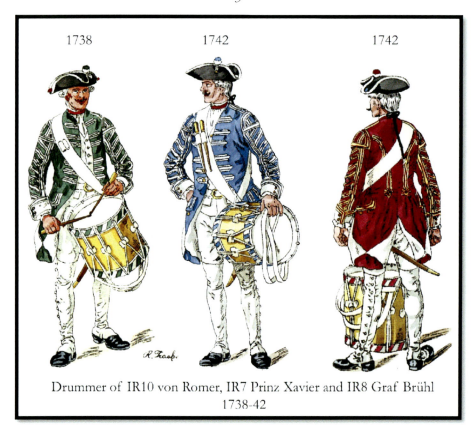

Drummer of IR10 von Romer, IR7 Prinz Xavier and IR8 Graf Brühl 1738-42

Infantry Uniform (1742-52)

IR6 von Freisen, 1748

HEADWEAR: Black tricorn laced white with white and yellow pompons.

STOCK: Red.

COAT: White arranged 1:2:3. The horizontal pockets had three buttons. Collar and cuffs with 3 buttons in facing colour. No shoulder straps or lapels.

WAISTCOAT: Waistcoat in facing colour with horizontal pockets and buttons.

LEGWEAR: In c1745, the breeches in facing colour were replaced by white buckskin breeches. Black or white gaiters and black shoes.

EQUIPMENT: Brown calfskin pack and haversack were carried with the tents in the baggage train. Black cartridge box with brass buckles, metalwork and white shoulder straps.

SIDEARMS: Troopers were armed with a musket, a bayonet and a sword. Musket covers were of black polished linen.

Table 3: Saxon Infantry Regiments 1742-52.

The white coats without collars & lapels. Breeches in facing colours until about 1745.

Regiment	coat	cuffs & turnbacks	lapels	waistcoat	buttons
IR1 *Königin* (1740)	white	cochineal red	none	cochineal red	brass
IR2 *Frankenberg* (1741) *Sachsen-Gotha* (1744)	white	sky blue [*bleumourant*]	none	sky blue [*bleumourant*]	brass
IR3 *Niesemeuschel* (1740) *von Frankenberg* (1746) *Prinz Friedrich* (1751)	white	yellow [*gelb*]	none	yellow [*gelb*]	brass
IR4 *Sach.-Weissenfels* (1702) *Prinz Clemens* (1746)	white	French blue [*franzblau*]	none	French blue [*franzblau*]	brass
IR5 *Sulkowski* (1737) *Alt Pirch* (1744) *von Minckwitz* (1746)	white	dark yellow [*orange gelb*]	none	dark yellow [*orange gelb*]	white metal
IR6 *von Kosel* (1739) *von Friese* (1746)	white	dark green [*dunkelgrün*]	none	dark green [*dunkelgrün*]	brass
IR7 *Prinz Xavier* (1733)	white	sky blue	none	sky blue	brass
IR8 (Est. 1741) *Graf Brühl* (1741)	white	poppy red cuffs & white turnbacks	none	poppy red	brass
IR9 *Stollberg-Rossla* (1742) *Lubomirski* (1752)	white	apple green cuffs & white turnbacks	none	apple green	brass
Fusilier Regt *von Schönberg* (1741) *Roccow* (1745)	green	red including collar	none	red	white metal
Disbanded in 1748					
IR10 (Est. 1680) *Römer* (1742) *Jung Pirch* (1744) *von Jasmund* (1746) Disbanded 1748	white	dark green [*dunkelgrün*]	none	dark green [*dunkelgrün*]	white metal
IR11 (Est 1702) *von Allnpeck* (1739) Disbanded 1748	white	French blue [*franzblau*]	none	French blue [*franzblau*]	white metal
IR12 (Raised 1742) *Bellegarde* (1742) Disbanded 1748	white	sky blue [*bleumourant*]	none	sky blue [*bleumourant*]	white metal

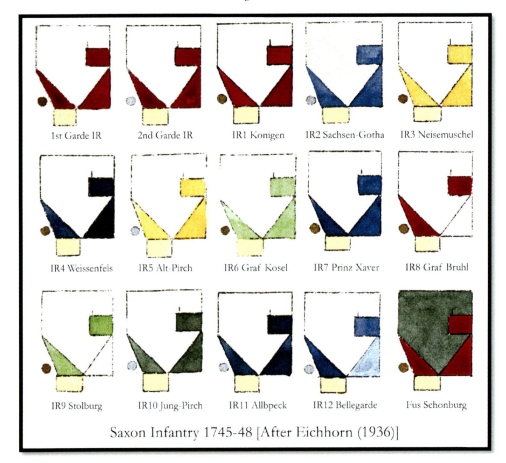

Saxon Infantry 1745-48 [After Eichhorn (1936)]

Infantry Uniform (1753-60)

HEADWEAR: Tricorns with white edging. Fatigue cap resembled the French *pokalem* were white with a band in facing colour and a tassel in the button colour. As these were made from old coats, there is unlikely to have been any uniformity.

COAT: White coat buttons arranged 1:2:3. The horizontal pockets had 3 buttons. Collar and cuffs with 3 buttons in facing colour. No shoulder straps or lapels. Turnbacks in facing colour fastened with a small button.

BARRACK DRESS: Grey sail cloth smocks and over-trousers for exercises and fatigue wear.

LEGWEAR: White or sometimes buff leather breeches were worn. White or black gaiters with brass buttons. Officers wore breeches in the facing colour.

GREATCOAT: A greatcoat [*Mantel*] in the coat colour was worn for guard duty.

EQUIPMENT: Black cartridge pouch with brass fittings. White leather straps with brass belt buckle. Brown calfskin pack and haversack were carried with the tents in the baggage train.

Table 4: Saxon Infantry Regiments 1753-61.[61]

Regiment	Coat	Collars, cuffs and turnbacks	Lapels	Waistcoat	Buttons
IR1 *Königin*	white	scarlet [*cochen.*]	none	scarlet [*cochen.*]	brass
IR2 *Sachsen-Gotha*	white	sky blue [*bleumourant*]	none	sky blue [*bleumourant*]	white metal
IR3 *Prinz Friedrich*	white	yellow [*gelb*]	none	yellow [*gelb*]	brass
IR4 *Prinz Clemens*	white	French blue [*franzblau*]	none	French blue [*franzblau*]	brass
IR5 *von Minckwitz*	white	French blue [*franzblau*]	none	French blue [*franzblau*]	white metal
IR6 *Maximilian*	white	Russian green [*russische grün*]	none	Russian green [*russische grün*]	brass
IR7 *Prinz Xaver*	white	sky blue [*bleumourant*]	sky blue [*bleumourant*]	sky blue [*bleumourant*]	brass
IR8 *Graf Brühl*	white	poppy red [*ponceaurot*]	poppy red [*ponceaurot*]	poppy red [*ponceaurot*]	brass
IR9 *Lubomirski*	white	yellow [*gelb*]	none	yellow [*gelb*]	white metal
Fus Regt *Rochow*	green	red [*rot*]	none	red [*rot*]	white metal

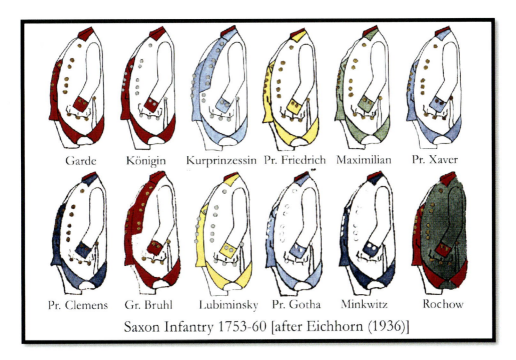

Saxon Infantry 1753-60 [after Eichhorn (1936)]

---

[61] Friedrich (1998) 23-26

SIDEARMS: The infantry short sword had a brass handle and ferrule, the scabbard was brown. Kurprinzessin and Graf Brühl carried a Pallasche. Kurprinzessin had red leather sabre straps.

TENTS: Tents were made of raw linen.

Officer Uniform

HEADWEAR: Black tricorn with lace in button colour and white cockade.

STOCK: White stock.

COAT: White coat did not have any lace and had ten buttons down the right hand side and corresponding buttonholes down the left.

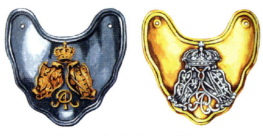

Saxon Officer's Gorget, c1740

DISTINCTIONS: The brass gorget with silver coat of arms was worn below the coat. Silver with crimson striped sash was tied on the right hand side.

HORSE FURNITURE: The saddlecloth was in facing colour with lace in the button colour: one band for lieutenants and two bands for captains and above.

NCO Uniform

HEADWEAR: Black tricorn with lace in button colour and white cockade.

STOCK: Red stock.

DISTINCTIONS: Corporals had one line of lace on cuffs and sergeants had two. IR Graf Brühl and Kurprinzessin Grenadier Bn also had lace on the turnbacks and lapels.

EQUIPMENT: Corporals wore their stick on the third button on the right. Fouriers wore their cartridge box on the front.

SIDEARMS: Corporals were armed with halberds and a pistol worn on the right hip. Fouriers were armed with muskets and pistols.

Musician Uniform

HEADWEAR: Black tricorn with lace in button colour and white cockade.

COAT: Coat in facing colour with lace in button colour and white turnbacks. For example IR Prinz Clemens had a dark blue coat with white facings. The sleeves had two thin stripes and chevrons in button colour. The buttonhole loops, pockets and the rosettes on the back of the coat was in buttonhole colour.

BELTS: White drum strap with two thin laces in facing colour.

EQUIPMENT: The brass drum had the twin shields of Poland and Saxony. The top and bottom band had alternating facing colour and button colour. The fife was in brass.

DISTINCTIONS: The Regimental Drum Major had thinner gold or silver lace according to the button colour and did not have a drum.

Infantry Uniform (1761-78)

HEADWEAR: Black tricorn laced white with white and yellow pompons. Fatigue cap similar to the French *"pokalem"* was white with facing colour lace around the edge and white tassel at the rear.

STOCK: Red stock.

COAT: White coat with horizontal pockets, each with three buttons. The collar and duffers were in facing colour. The cuffs had three buttons. The lapels had eight buttons arranged 2:2:2:2 and three more on the coat below the lapel. The turnbacks in facing colour were fastened with a small button. No shoulder straps.

Table 5: Saxon Infantry Regiments 1761-78

Regiment	Coat colour	Collar, cuffs & turnbacks	Lapels	Waistcoat	Buttons
IR1 *Prinz Joseph*	white	deep red	deep red	deep red	yellow
IR2 *Sachsen-Gotha*	white	light blue	light blue	light blue	yellow
IR3 *Prinz Friedrich*	white	yellow	yellow	yellow	yellow
IR4 *Prinz Clemens*	white	dark blue	dark blue	dark blue	yellow
IR5 *von Minckwitz*	white	dark blue	dark blue	dark blue	white
IR6 *Maximilian*	white	dark green	dark green	dark green	yellow
IR7 *Prinz Xavier*	white	sky blue	sky blue	sky blue	yellow
IR8 *Graf Brühl*	white	red	red	red	yellow
IR9 *Lubomirski*	white	yellow	yellow	yellow	white
Fus Regt *Rochow*	green	scarlet	scarlet	scarlet	white

WAISTCOAT: Waistcoat was in the facing colour with horizontal pockets.
LEGWEAR: White breeches, black gaiters and black shoes.
SIDEARMS: Troopers were armed with a musket, a bayonet and a sword mainly of French or Austrian manufacture.

Officer Uniform – As before.

NCO Uniform

HEADWEAR: Black tricorn with lace in button colour and white cockade.

DISTINCTIONS: Corporals had one line of lace on cuffs and sergeants had two. Also had lace on the turnbacks and lapels.

IR6 Maximilian (1761-78)   IR1 Prinz Joseph (1761-63)

[Wilhelm Dietrich, 1907]

Musicians

HEADWEAR: Tricorn with white edging, white cockade and plume that varied according to the regiment.

DISTINCTIONS: Coats in facing colour and the lace in button colour.

Chapter 5: Saxon Grenadier

It was common practice throughout the period to converge the two grenadier companies from two regiments into Grenadier Battalions. The exception was the Bellegard Grenadier Battalion renamed Kurprinzessin in 1750 that was a grenadier battalion in its own write. In 1756, during the containment of the Saxon army at Lilienstein the grenadier companies from two regiments were combined, except the Grenadier Bn Kurprinzessin. A grenadier company had the following had 1 *Kapitän*, 1 *Premierleutnant*, 2 *Sous-Leutnant*, 3 *Sergeanten*, 1 *Fourier*, 1 *Feldscher*, 5 *Korporale*, 2 *Pfeifer*, 3 *Tamboure*, 2 *Zimmerleute*, 76 *Grenadiere*. [See OOB 13]

OOB 13: Grenadier Battalions formed in 1756.[62]

Grenadier-Bn Bennigsen: [red facings]
   Formed from the grenadiers of *Garde zu Fuss* & IR8 *Graf Brühl*.
Grenadier-Bn Kavanagh: [yellow mitre bags]
   Formed from the grenadiers of IR3 *Prinz Friedrich August* & IR9 *Lubomirski*.
Grenadier-Bn von de Pforte: [sky blue mitre bags]
   Formed from the grenadiers of IR2 *Prinz Saxe-Gotha* & IR7 *Prince Xaver*.
Grenadier-Bn von Götze: [French blue mitre bags]
   Formed from the grenadiers of IR5 *Minckwitz*. IR6 *Maximilian*
Grenadier-Bn von Milckau: [red facings]
   Formed from the grenadiers of IR1 *Königin* & Fus *von Rochow*.
Grenadier-Bn von Pfundheller: [French blue and red/*paille* facings]
   Formed from the grenadiers of IR4 *Prince Clemens* & *Leib-Grenadier-Garde*.
Grenadier Bn von Kurprinzessin [sky blue facings]

In March 1757, the Prussians formed five combined grenadier battalions from the disbanded Saxon grenadier battalions. [See OOB 14.]

OOB 14: Prussian Grenadier Battalions formed in March 1756.[63]

Gren-Bn S50/S58 von Bähr	[Disbanded 30 July 1757]
Gren-Bn S51/S59 von Bornstedt	[Disbanded 5 Aug 1757]
Gren-Bn S52/S55 von Kahlenberg	[Disbanded 30 July 1757]
Gren-Bn S53/S57 von Dieselsky	[Disbanded 14 Nov 1757]
Gren-Bn S54/S56 von Köller	[2 July 1761-1763 *von Rothkirch*]

In 1757, the Kurprinzessin Regiment was expanded to a two battalions when it was reformed in Hungary.

---

[62] Schirmer (1989) III-2
[63] Bleckwenn (1987) IV: 73

Kurprinzessin-Grenadier-Battalion

Formed in 1748 from the grenadier companies of the disbanded 2nd Garde, IR10 Jasmund, IR11 Allnpeck and IR12 Bellegarde. In 1749, the eight companies were reduced to five companies. In 1756, the regiment consisted of five grenadier companies (539 men). In 1756, the regiment became prisoners at Pirna. In 1757, the regiment of two battalions was reformed in Hungary from among the rallied *Referenten* and new recruits drawn from Bavaria. It served with the Saxon auxiliary corps with the French until 1763. When it returned to Saxony, the regiment was converted into an infantry regiment with three battalions in fourteen companies. However, the regiment retained their grenadier sabres and the privilege to play the *Grenadiermarsch*. In 1778, it was reduced to two battalions of ten companies.

Grenadier Bn von Bellegarde Officer (1748-50)

Inhaber
Grenadier Battalion
1748 *Bellegarde-Grenadiere Bn*[64]
1750 *Kurprinzessin-Gren Bn* [Disbanded 1756]
1757 [New] *Kurprinzessin-Regiment*
Infantry Regiment
1763 [New] *Kurprinzessin*
1781 *Benningsen*
1784 *Reitzenstein*
1790 *Wolffersdorff*
1791 *Heyde*
1800 *Brause*
1800 *Ryssel*
1805 *Bünau*
1806 *Bevilaqua*
1808 *von Dyherrn*
1810 Disbanded

Commander
1750 *Oberst von Klingenberg*
1756 *Oberst von Flemming*[65]

Staff: 1 *Oberst-Leutnant*, 1 *Major*, 1 *Regiments-Quartiermeister*, 1 *Adjutant*, 1 *Regiments-Feldscher*, 6 *Hoboisten*, 1 *Regiments-Tambour*, 4 *Pfeifer*, 1 *Profos*, 1 *Knecht*.

Five Companies: 1 *Kapitän*, 1 1st Lt, 1 2nd Lt, 3 *Sergeanten*, 1 *Gefreiten-Korporal*, 1 *Fourier*, 1 *Feldscher*, 5 *Korporale*, 3 *Tamboure*, 2 *Zimmerleute*, 86 *Grenadiere*.

---

[64] *GM Entremont de Bellegarde*
[65] He became general inspector of the infantry in 1768.

Uniform 1748-53

HEADWEAR: Grenadier wore the Prussian style mitre cap. Officers and NCOs wore a black tricorn laced silver with a white cockade.
STOCK: Red.
COAT: White coat with sky blue lapels and no shoulder straps.
COLLAR and CUFFS: Sky blue.
TURNBACKS: Sky blue.
WAISTCOAT: Sky blue.

Uniform 1753-56

HEADWEAR: Grenadier wore the Prussian style mitre cap until 1756 when they received the tricorn. Officers and NCOs wore a black tricorn laced silver with a white cockade.
STOCK: Red.
COAT: White coat with sky blue lapels and no shoulder straps.
COLLAR and CUFFS: Sky blue.
TURNBACKS: Sky blue.
WAISTCOAT: Sky blue.
BUTTONS: White metal (2:2:2).

Uniform (1761-70)

HEADWEAR: Grenadiers and NCOs wore black fur bearskin (Austrian style) with a white metal plate with the electoral crest; falling from the rear of the bearskin were white woollen cords and tassels, the latter with the inner part in mid blue. Officers wore a black fur bearskin with gilt plate with the electoral crest and mid blue bag with golden cords and tassels.
UNIFORM: As above.

Kurprinzessin-Grenadier Battalion (1753-63)

Campaign History

In 1756, part of von Crousaz's 1st Grenadier Brigade. The grenadiers refused to take the oath to the King of Prussia so the men were distributed among the Prussian infantry regiments. The reformed regiment was part of the Saxon Auxiliary Corps that operated with the French (1758-63).[66]

---

[66] Anon (1887) *Geschichte des Koenigliche Saechsische 6. Infanterie-Regiments No 105*, Leipzig, 418

Grenadier Uniform

Investigation of the type of grenadier caps that was worn by the Saxon Infantry is confusing and contradictory.

Grenadiers (1735-42)

HEADWEAR: Prussian fusilier cap replaced the earlier felt mitre cap. The latter had a bag hanging down behind in the regimental facing colour with a red shield trimmed gold.

UNIFORM: As musketeers.

EQUIPMENT: Difference in ammunition pouch. In addition to cartridge box grenadiers had a small box on the waist-belt.

Grenadiers of the *Leib-Garde zu Fuss*, 1738-41 [after Trache]

Grenadier Officer, NCO and Grenadier of the
Leib-Garde zu Fuss in parade uniform, 1738-41

Grenadiers (1743-55)

It was instructed on 1 June 1756 that all fusilier caps would be replaced by grenadier caps.

HEADWEAR: Grenadiers wore the fusilier cap and some may have worn the Prussian style earlier than 1756.[67] *Ad Interim*, the grenadiers lead also wore tricorns with white curve edgings.

UNIFORM: As musketeers.

EQUIPMENT: As above.

---

[67] The grenadier of the Leib-Grenadier-Garde and the Kurprinzessin Grenadier-Bn are shown with the Grenadier Cap in Meissen contemporary porcelain figures dating from about 1750. [Schirmer (1989: III-1) quoting Knötel] Yet Eichhorn showed an officer of the Kurprinzessin Grenadier Bn in a fusilier mitre in 1753. [Pengel and Hurt (1981)]

Grenadiers (1756)

HEADWEAR: Grenadier mitre with brass or white metal front-plate. Unlike Prussian grenadier caps, the headband was normally brass (IR3, IR4 and IR7) or white metal (IR2, IR5, IR6, IR8 and IR9). The exception was IR1 in the facing colour. The bag was normally in facing colour with complimentary piping. The pompom was distinctive for each regiment. *Ad Interim*, the grenadiers lead also wore tricorns with white curve edgings.

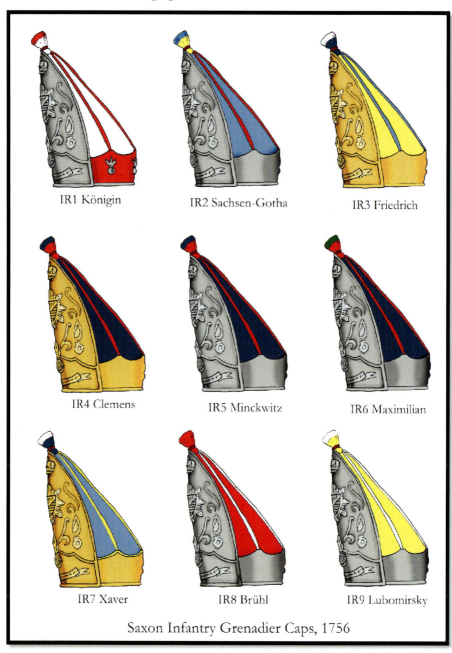

Saxon Infantry Grenadier Caps, 1756

Table 6: Saxon Infantry Grenadier caps (c1756).[68]

Regiment	Front Plate	Pompom	Bag	Base	Lace
IR1 *Königin*	white metal	red-white	white	Red with white grenades	red
IR2 *Sachsen-Gotha*	white metal	yellow-sky blue	*bleumourant* [sky blue]	white metal	white
IR3 *Friedrich*	brass	white-blue	yellow	brass	*bleumourant* [sky blue]
IR4 *Clemens*	brass	dark blue-red	dark blue	brass	red
IR5 *Minckwitz*	white metal	dark blue-red	dark blue	white metal	red
IR6 *Maximilian*	white metal	dark green-red	dark blue	white metal	red
IR7 *Xaver*	brass	white-blue	*bleumourant* [sky blue]	brass	yellow
IR8 *Brühl*	white metal	red	red	white metal	white
IR9 *Lubomirski*	white metal	white-yellow	yellow	white metal	white

Table 7: *Kurprinzessin* wore grenadier caps and fusilier caps (c1756).[69]

Regiment	Front Plate	Pompom	Bag	Base	Lace
Kurprinzessin Bn Grenadier Cap	white metal	white	sky blue	blue with white grenades	white
Kurprinzessin Bn Fusilier Cap	brass	none	black	black with brass hoops	brass bugle

Table 8: Saxon Guard Grenadier mitre caps (c1756).[70]

Regiment	Front Plate	Pompom	Bag	Base	Lace
I/*Leib-Garde-Grenadier*	white metal	red-yellow	lemon	white metal	red
II/*Leib-Garde-Grenadier*	brass	yellow	lemon	brass	white
Garde zu Fuss	white metal	dark red	dark red	white metal	white

---

[68] Schirmer (1989) III-4
[69] Schirmer (1989) III-4
[70] Schirmer (1989) III-4

The Leib-Grenadier-Garde also wore a black leather cap with a brass star, edging and ornaments instead of the tricorn.[71] This probably dated from the 1740s.

Leib-Grenadier Cap, 1740

Table 9: The Fusilier Regiment Roccow wore the fusilier cap (1742-56).[72]

Regiment	Front Plate	Large Pompom	Bag	Base	Lace
Fus Regt *Roccow*	white metal	dark green-red	dark green	white metal	red

Grenadier Sabre

18th Century Infantry Sabre

---

[71] Schirmer (1989) III-4
[72] Schirmer (1989) III-4

Grenadier Uniform (1757-60)

HEADGEAR: Grenadier black tricorn laced scalloped white lace.
UNIFORM: As given in Table 10.

Table 10: Grenadier company uniforms (1757-60)

Grenadier Coy	Coat	Collars & cuffs	Lapels	Turnbacks	Waistcoat	Buttons
Formed from former member of the Saxon Artillery. In July 1758, these grenadier companies formed the artillery detachments armed with 4pdr "*à la Suédoise*" regimental guns donated by Princess Maria Josepha of Saxony, the wife of Louis, Dauphin of France.						
IR2 *Sachsen-Gotha*	green [*grün*]	red [*rot*]	red [*rot*]	red [*rot*]	*paille*	brass
IR9 *Lubomirski*	green [*grün*]	red [*rot*]	red [*rot*]	red [*rot*]	*paille*	brass
Formed from former members of the Garde du Corps and in 1761 formed the *Reiter* Regiment.						
IR4 *Prinz Clemens*	light red	blue [*blau*]	none	light blue [*hellblau*]	*paille*	brass
IR8 *Brühl*	light red	blue [*blau*]	none	light blue [*hellblau*]	*paille*	brass
Formed from former members of the six cuirassier regiments and in 1761 formed the *Reiter* Regiment.						
IR5 *von Minckwitz*	white	blue [*blau*]	none	light blue [*hellblau*]	*paille*	white metal
Fus Regt *Rochow*	white	green [*grün*]	none	green [*grün*]	*paille*	white metal
In 1761, these formed the *Leib-Grenadier Battalion*.						
IR1 *Prinz Joseph*	light red	yellow [*gelb*]	yellow [*gelb*]	yellow [*gelb*]	yellow [*gelb*]	white metal
IR6 *Maximilian*	light red	yellow [*gelb*]	yellow [*gelb*]	yellow [*gelb*]	yellow [*gelb*]	white metal
These regiments retained their grenadiers throughout the seven years war.						
Kurprinzessin IR	white	blue [*blau*]	blue [*blau*]	light blue [*hellblau*]	blue [*blau*]	white metal
IR3 *Friedrich August*	white	yellow	none	yellow [*gelb*]	yellow [*gelb*]	brass
IR7 *Xaver*	white	light blue [*hellblau*]	none	blue [*blau*]	blue [*blau*]	brass

~ 87 ~

Saxon Army 1740-1763

Grenadier of IR Prinz Clemens, 1761-78

Uniform (1761-78)

In 1761, when all twelve infantry regiments were re-organised into four musketeer companies plus one grenadier company, the grenadiers were formed into the Leib-Grenadier Garde Battalion and two Field-Grenadier-Battalions.

HEADWEAR: Grenadiers and NCOs wore a black Austrian style fur bearskin with a brass plate with the electoral crest; falling from the rear of the bearskin were white woollen cords and tassels, the latter with a yellow inner part. Officers wore Austrian style black fur bearskin with a gilt plate with the electoral crest and yellow bag with golden cords and tassels.

Grenadier Cap, 1761

Officer's Grenadier cap (left) and Grenadier cap, 1761

Leib-Grenadier Garde Battalion

Officer in full dress

Officer

Grenadier in undress

Grenadier in full dress

Leib-Grenadier-Garde, 1761-90
[Wilhelm Dietrich, 1907]

HEADWEAR: Bearskin hat with brass plate. A tricorn with curved white edging was worn when not in full dress.

STOCK: Red stock.

COAT: Red coat with yellow collar, cuffs and turnbacks. White fringed epaulettes were worn on both shoulders.

LAPELS: Yellow.

WAISTCOAT: Yellow waistcoat.

BUTTONS: White metal.

LEGWEAR: Yellow breeches, white or black gaiters and black shoes.

Leib-Grenadier-Garde, 1761-90
[Wilhelm Dietrich, 1907]

OFFICERS: As grenadiers but with sash, black stock and armed with musket with special partizan bladed bayonet.

MUSICIANS: Yellow coat with blue facings and white lace. Blue waistcoat with white lace. Blue breeches, white gaiters and black shoes.

NCOs: Silver lace to collar, cuffs and lapels plus a swagger stick.

Chapter 6: Kreis Regiments

On 21 January 1733 August the Strong re-established the land militia that was now known as *Kreis-Regiment* [Circle Regiment]. Each *Kreis-Regiment* was formed into two battalions. Only small cadres were maintained in peacetime and they were not fully mobilised in 1756.

In 1741, the 3rd and 4th *Kreis Regiment* were mobilised. In 1743 all four regiments were deployed. In 1745, after the battle of Kesselsdorf, Friedrich II in Dresden drafted 3000 *Kreis* troops into his Prussian army. Until 1752 the *Kreis-Regiments* were drilled for two 14 day periods in the summer and autumn.

From 1752 a battalion of the *Kreis* troops was assigned to each field regiment during exercises.

OOB 15: Headquarters and commanders of the four *Kreis-Regiments*.[73]

	Headquarters	Commanders
1. *Kreis-Regiment*	Weissenfels	1733 *von Schlichting* 1748-56 *von Sternstein*
2. *Kreis-Regiment*	Oschatz	1733 *von Metzradt* 1748-56 *von Pflugk*
3. *Kreis-Regiment*	Bautzen	1733 *von Zschertwitz* 1742 *von Rogucki* 1756 *von Schönberg*
4. *Kreis-Regiment*	Freiberg	1733-56 *von Brüchting*

In 1748, the *Kreis-Regiment* had the following organisation. Each 2000 strong *Kreis-Regiment* was split into four grenadier and eight musketeer company. It was divided in three battalions.

Staff (7 officers): 1 *Oberst*, 1 *Oberst-Lt*, 2 majors, 2 adjutants and 1 *Auditeur*.

Twelve Companies: 12 captains, 12 first lieutenants, 12 second lieutenants, 24 sergeants, 4 *Fahnen-Junker*, 12 *Fourier*, 70 corporals, 24 drummers, 600 grenadiers and 1972 musketeers.

The *Kreis-Regiments* virtually came to their end in 1756 with the dissolving of the Saxon army. Already after 1754, vacancies were not filled. The regiments were formally disbanded in 1763.

---

[73] Hasse & Eichhorn (1936) 13

Uniform (1734-44)

HEADWEAR: Black tricorn with white lace were won from 4 May 1734.

STOCK: Black stock.

COAT: Red coat with horizontal pockets, each with 3 buttons. Blue collar and cuffs without cuff button. No lapels or shoulder straps. Turnbacks in facing colour fastened with a small button.

WAISTCOAT: Facing colour with horizontal pockets and white metal buttons.

BUTTONS: White metal.

LEGWEAR: From 3 May 1734, white breeches, black canvas gaiters and black shoes were worn. The breeches became blue from 1740.

EQUIPMENT: White belt with brass fittings, bayonet and sheath.

Table 11: Saxon Circle Regiments (1733-45)

Regiment	Coat colour	Facings	Buttons
1. Kreis Regt. *von Schlichting* (1733)	red	blue	white metal
2. Kreis Regt. *von Pflügk* (1733)	red	dark blue	white metal
3. Kreis Regt. *von Ragouski* (1733)	red	white	white metal
4. Kreis Regt. *von Brüchting* (1733)	red	blue	white metal

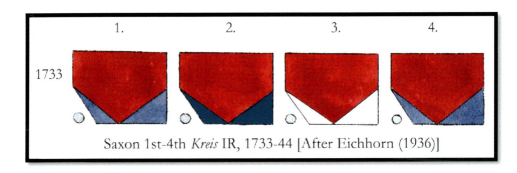

Saxon 1st-4th *Kreis* IR, 1733-44 [After Eichhorn (1936)]

Saxon Army 1740-1763

Corporal — Officer

1st (left) and 2nd (right) Kreise Infantry Regiment, 1748-63 [Trache]

Uniform (1745-63)

On 15 February 1745 the coat changed from red to a white coat with collar, cuffs, turnbacks and waistcoat in facing colour.

HEADWEAR: Black tricorn with white lace.

STOCK: Black stock.

COAT: Grey coat with horizontal pockets, each with 3 buttons. Collar and cuffs in facing colour. The cuff did not have a button. No lapels or shoulder straps. Facing colour fastened with a small button.

WAISTCOAT: Facing colour with horizontal pockets and white metal buttons.

BUTTONS: White metal buttons in 1, 2 3 formation.

LEGWEAR: Straw coloured breeches, black gaiters and black shoes.

EQUIPMENT: White belt with brass fittings, bayonet and sheath.

SIDEARMS: Troopers were armed with a musket, a bayonet and a sword.

DISTINCTIONS: Corporals carried a halberd and pistol on the right shoulder and a sword.

Table 12: Saxon Circle Regiments (1745-63)

Regiment	Coat colour	Facings	Buttons	Breeches
1. Kreis Regt. *von Schlichting* (1733) *von Sternstein* (1748)	pike grey	yellow	white metal	Straw
2. Kreis Regt. *von Pflügk* (1733)	pike grey	light blue	white metal	Straw
3. Kreis Regt. *von Rogucki* (1742) *von Schönberg* (1756)	pike grey	red	white metal	Straw
4. Kreis Regt. *von Brüchting* (1733)	pike grey	green	white metal	Straw

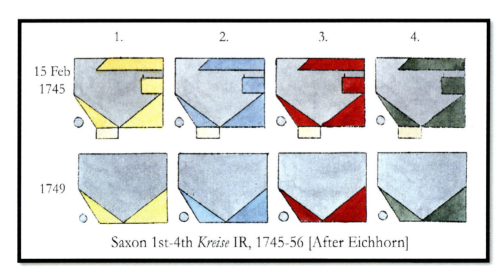

Saxon 1st-4th *Kreise* IR, 1745-56 [After Eichhorn]

Saxon Army 1740-1763

Grenadier Drummer

Saxon 3rd Kreis Infantry Regiment, 1748-63 [Trache]

Saxon Army 1740-1763

Corporal Musketeer

4th Saxon Kreis Infantry Regiment, 1748-56

Chapter 7:
Infantry Flags

Before union of Saxony and Poland in 1697, the infantry flags matched the facing colours without decoration, or embroidered flames in the corners and a green wreath in the middle. The finial had the "*FAC*" cipher. After the union between Saxony and Poland, the flags had the crowned monogram "*FARP*" framed by two palm leaves was on both sides of the flag whose field was in the facing colours. The diagonal and middle of the four sides had embroidered flames in button colour.

Saxon Infantry Leibfahne (left) and Ordinärfahne (right), c1710

M1732 Infantry Flags

In 1732, new infantry flags had a crown and the "*AR*" cipher enclosed within palm leaves on the field of the facing colour. The exceptions were the 1st & 2nd Garde IR with white flags and IR10 *Marche* with carmine red [*karmoisinrote*] flags.

IR2 Hauxhausen, c1730   IR3 Du Caila, c1730

Grenadier Bn Kurprinzessin 1732-53 [Hottenroth (1910)]

Leibfahne — Ordinärefahne

IR7 Sachsen-Weimar, c1730

The other exception was the flag of IR7 Saxon-Weimar of grass-green cloth and cipher "EA" for Ernst August on a pedestal under the prince's crown, framed by palm leaves.

With the accession of Elector Friedrich August II of Saxony (King August III of Poland), he retained this design and some of the newly issued flags had the Arabian "3" in the cipher. The allocation of flags was a mess due to losses during the Austrian War of Succession and the subsequent dissolution of many regiments. The flag colours often did not agree with the facings, even within a battalion the flags were often different colours.

M1753 Infantry Flags

It was not until 1753 at the Camp of Übigau that August III was in a position to replace all the infantry flags. The M1753 flags were identical on both sides. Infantry regiments carried four flags, one *Leibfahne* and three *Ordinarfahne*. The first battalion carried the *Leibfahne* and one *Ordinarfahne*. The second battalion carried two *Ordinarfahne*. Saxon infantry flags were 186cm by 158cm. Both sides were embroidered on a separate sheet of taffeta silk and sewn together. The staves were covered with poppy red cloth attached with silver or gold plated nails according to the button colour of the regiment. The finials and ferrules were gilt.

The white *Leibfahne* had a coat of arms and cipher. The regiments were distinguished by different coloured borders.

The *Ordinärfahnen* in the facing colour had a crowned "*AR*" cipher in gold on a white pedestal. This was surrounded by a wreath of pale green branches tied with golden ribbons. The border was white, yellow or red with white or yellow depending upon the regiment.

Table 13: Summary of M1753 flags of the Saxon *Garde*.
Where [H] = Hottenroth (1910), [L] = Lange (1981) and [B] = Brentnall (2011)

Regiment	Type	Field	Border	Piping
Leib Grenadier Garde	Leibfahne	White	Yellow [L]	Red [B]
	Ordinarfahne[74]	Yellow [H]	Red [L]	White [B]
Garde zu Fuss	Leibfahne	White	Red [L]	Yellow [B]
	Ordinarfahne	Red [H]	White [B]	Yellow [B]
Grenadier Kurprinzessin	Leibfahne	White	Bleumourant [L]	Yellow [B]
	Ordinarfahne	Bleumourant [H]	White [L]	Yellow [L]

---

[74] This Yellow *Ordinarfahne* was in *Leibfahne* pattern. [Brentnall (2011) *Personal Communication*.

Garde zu Fuss Flags

Table 14: Saxon M1753 infantry flags.[75]

Where [H] = Hottenroth (1910), [L] = Lange (1981) and [B] = Brentnall (2011)

Regiment	Type	Field	Border	Piping
IR1	*Leibfahne*	White	Cochineal [L]	Yellow [B]
Königin	*Ordinarfahne*	Cochineal [H]	White [L]	Yellow [L]
IR2	*Leibfahne*	White	Bleumourant [L]	Yellow [B]
Sachsen-Gotha	*Ordinarfahne*	Bleumourant [H]	White [L]	Yellow [L]
IR3	*Leibfahne*	White	Yellow [L]	Red [B]
Prinz Friedrich	*Ordinarfahne*	Yellow [H]	Red [H]	White [H]
IR4	*Leibfahne*	White	Dark Blue [L]	Yellow [B]
Prinz Clemens	*Ordinarfahne*	Dark Blue [H]	Yellow [L]	White [L]
IR5	*Leibfahne*	White	Dark Blue [L]	Yellow [B]
Minckwitz	*Ordinarfahne*	Dark Blue [H]	White [L]	Yellow [L]
IR6	*Leibfahne*	White	Green [L]	Red [B]
Maximilian	*Ordinarfahne*	Green [H]	White [L]	Red [L]
IR7	*Leibfahne*	White	Bleumourant [L]	Yellow [B]
Prinz Xavier	*Ordinarfahne*	Bleumourant [H]	White [L]	Yellow [L]
IR8	*Leibfahne*	White	Ponceau [L]	Yellow [B]
Graf Brühl	*Ordinarfahne*	Ponceau [H]	Yellow [L]	White [L]
IR9	*Leibfahne*	White	Yellow [L]	Red [B]
Lubomirski	*Ordinarfahne*	Yellow [H]	White [B]	Red [B]
Füs. Regt.	*Leibfahne*	White	Dark *Ponceau* [L]	Yellow [B]
Rochow	*Ordinarfahne*	Dark *Ponceau* [H]	White [B]	Yellow [B]

---

[75] [Andrew Brentnall (2011) *Private Communication*]

Saxon Army 1740-1763

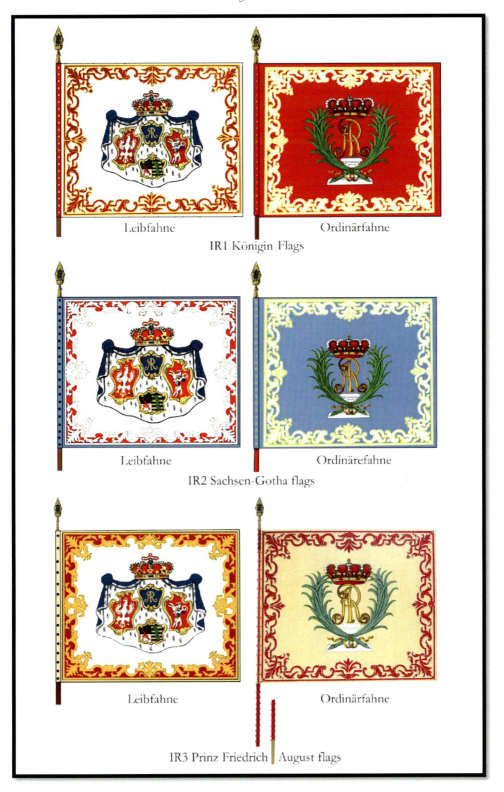

Saxon Army 1740-1763

Saxon Army 1740-1763

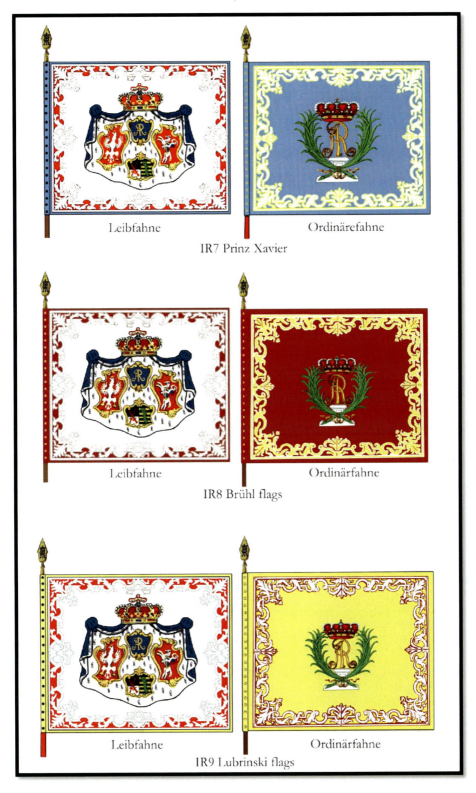

Leibfahne — Ordinärfahne
Füs. Regt. Rochow

M1758 Saxon Infantry Fags

Ordinärfahne of Grenadier Bn Kurprincessin, c1754

In March 1758, the twelve reformed infantry regiments in Hungary were issued flags by the Austrian government in the same proportion as before. These had been produced in Vienna from taffeta silk with the emblems and decorations in oils as were Austrian infantry flags. These flags were not durable and were replaced in 1763-66 by the M1753 flags that had been laid up in Königstein in 1756.

It was only on 30 May 1785 at the camp at Mühlberg that new flags were issued and the old ones placed in the *Hauptzeughaus*. Finally, the Polish coat of arms disappeared from the Saxon flags. These painted flags had the coats of arms on a pedestal framed by palm leaves. However, these painted flags proved fragile and therefore it was decided that they would be replaced with embroidered ones again. The border of the flags served for the differentiation of the regiments. In September 1802, the infantry were issued new flags.

Chapter 8: Saxon Cuirassier

The Cuirassier Regiment of 1717-35 had six cuirassier companies (83 men each) and a *Karabinier* company (71 men) giving a total strength of 580 men.[76] The *Karabinier* Company was formed from drafts from the other six cuirassier companies.

In 1730, the Saxon army had four cuirassier regiments [KR1 *Königlicher Prinz/Kronprinz*, KR2 *Prinz Friedrich*, KR3 *von Polenz* and "KR-iv" *von Kriegern*]. In 1731, the "KR-vi" *Graf Nassau* was formed. In 1732 the "KR-v" *Graf Promnitz* was formed from drafts from the other five cuirassier regiments chiefly from dissolving their Karabinier companies. The "KR-vii" *von Brand* was formed from the Grenadier companies from the four dragoon regiments. In 1733 the *Grenadier a Cheval* were converted into the "KR-viii" *Sachsen-Gotha*.

The authorized strength of the cuirassier regiment from 1733 was 351 men. This consisted of the regimental staff and two squadrons each of two companies.

In 1733 Cuirassier Regiments were reduced to four companies and the *Karabinier* Company dissolved. Total strength was now 351 all ranks.[77]

Regimental staff (11 men):
1 *Oberst*, 1 major, 1 *Regiments-Quartiermeister*, 1 Adjutant, 1 *Auditeur*, 1 *Feldprediger*, 1 *Wagenmeister*, 1 *Regiments-Feldscher*, 1 *Pauker*, 1 *Profos*, 1 *Knecht* (driver).

Four Companies (4 companies of 85 = 340 men):
4 *Rittmeister*, 4 *Premier-Lt*, 4 *Sous-Lt*, 4 *Kornet*, 8 *Wachtmeister*, 4 *Standart-Junker*, 4 *Feldscher*, 4 *Fourier*, 16 corporals, 8 trumpeters and 280 troopers.

During the War of Austrian Succession, each Saxon Cuirassier Regiment had three squadrons of two companies of 95 all ranks giving 621 mounted men. In the field, the strength was much smaller and many could not field more than 200 troopers.[78] Saxon cavalry formed up in two or three ranks. Each squadron was divided into 3 sections, each with 2 half-sections. Although the use of firearms while mounted had been practised, instructions called for charging at a gallop and relying on "cold steel" only. Each cavalry regiment had 33 wagons and 150 horses.

---

[76] Hasse and Eichhorn (1936) 4
[77] Hasse and Eichhorn (1936) 4
[78] Manley (1998) 20

In 1746 "KR-vii" *L'Annonciade* was disbanded. In 1748, the eight cuirassier regiments and four dragoon regiments were reduced to six cuirassier regiments. "KR-iv" *von Ronnow*, "KR-v" *O'Byrn*, "KR-vi" *von Minkwitz* and "KR-viii" *von Dallwitz* were disbanded. DR1 *von Rechenberg*, DR3 *von Arnim* and DR4 *von Plötz* were converted into Cuirassier Regiments. DR2 *von Sondershausen* became part of KR *von Vitzthum*.

In 1748, Cuirassier Regiments were increased to eight companies. This gave a strength of 601 all ranks.[79]

Regimental staff (9 men):
1 *Oberst*, 1 *Oberst-Lt*, 1 *Major*, 1 *Regiments-Quartiermeister*, 1 Adjutant, 1 *Auditeur*, 1 *Regiments-Feldscher*, 1 *Pauker*, 1 *Profos*.

Eight Companies (8 x 74 men = 592 men):
8 *Rittmeister*, 8 Lt, 8 *Kornet*, 16 *Wachtmeister*, 8 *Standart-Junker*, 8 *Feldscher*, 8 *Fourier*, 32 corporals, 16 trumpeters and 480 troopers.

According to the 1753 Regulations, the peacetime establishment for each cuirassier regiment was four squadrons for a total of 514 men and 394 horses.

All six cuirassier regiments and the Garde du Corps were captured at Pirna in October 1756. The remnants that escaped from Prussian service were formed into Grenadier companies for the reformed infantry regiments. In 1761, these were formed into the *Reuter* Regiment. It was not until 1763 that the cuirassier regiments were reformed.

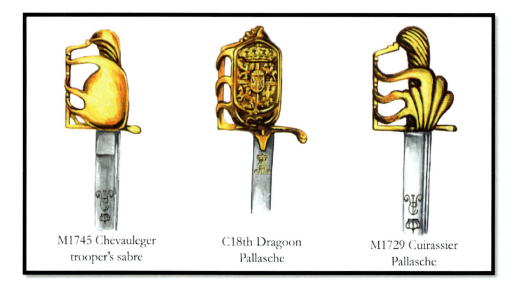

M1745 Chevauleger trooper's sabre C18th Dragoon Pallasche M1729 Cuirassier Pallasche

---

[79] Hasse and Eichhorn (1936) 4

The "Old" Cuirassier Regiments

KR1 Leib-Cuirassier Regiment (1680-1806)

The regiment was raised in 1680 as a Cavalry Regiment. It became a Cuirassier Regiment in 1697. The regiment capitulated to the Prussians in 1756. In 1763, a new KR1 *Leib-Regiment* was formed.

Inhaber
Cavalry Regiment
1680 *Promnitz zu Pferde*
1682 *von Plotho*
1689 *von Haubitz*
1692 *von Rathsamshausen*
1695 *Graf Reuss*
Cuirassier Regiment
1697 *Graf Trautmansdorff*
1699 *La Forest*
1700 *Kurprinz*
1713 *Königlicher Prinz*
1726 *Kronprinz*
1733 *Leib-Regiment*
1756 Disbanded
1763 [New] *Leib-Regiment*
1764 *Kurfürst*
1806 *König*
1807 *Leib-Kürassier-Garde*

Commander
c1756 *Oberst von Reitzenstein*

Uniform (1740-48)
HEADWEAR: Plain black tricorn with scarlet pom-pom.
STOCKS: Red.
COAT: White coat with light blue facings.
WAISTCOAT: The collarless light buff [*Lederkoller*] waistcoat with light blue edging was worn on field service beneath the cuirass. Light blue cuffs edged yellow. Light blue turnbacks.
FACINGS: Light blue.
BUTTONS: Brass.
CUIRASS: Black lacquered cuirass line with scarlet cloth.
LEGWEAR: Buff breeches.

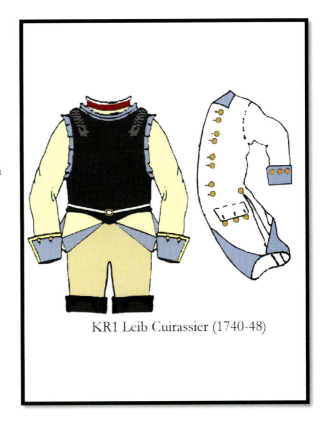

KR1 Leib Cuirassier (1740-48)

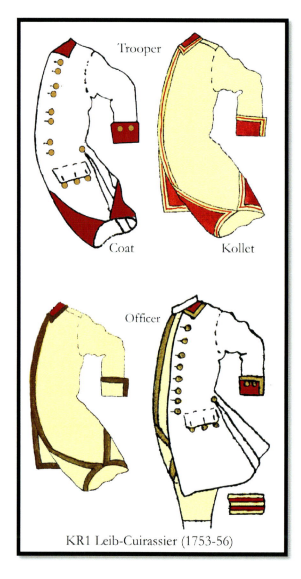

Uniform (1748-56)
In 1748, the facings were changed to scarlet.

HEADWEAR: Plain black tricorn with scarlet pom-pom.

COAT: White coat with scarlet collar, cuffs with two brass buttons and turnbacks.

BUTTONS: Brass (2:2:2:2)

WAISTCOAT: The collarless light buff [*Lederkoller*] waistcoat with scarlet edging was worn on field service beneath the cuirass. Scarlet cuffs edged yellow. Scarlet edging to the turnbacks.

FACINGS: Scarlet.

BUTTONS: Brass.

CUIRASS: Black lacquered cuirass line with scarlet cloth.

LEGWEAR: Scarlet breeches until 1753 then buff breeches.

Saxon Army 1740-1763

Farrier of the KR1 Leib-Cuirassier Regiment, 1748-56
[After Trache]

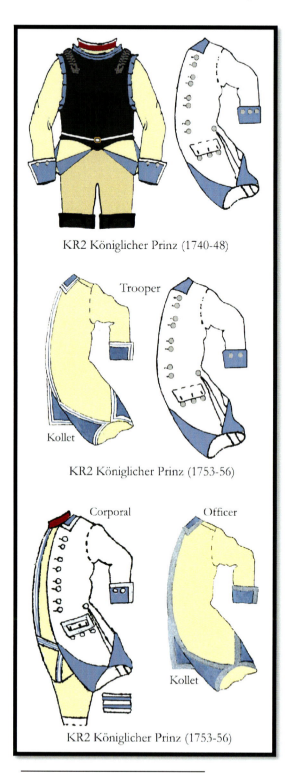

KR2 Königlicher Prinz (1703-78)

The regiment was formed in 1703 as a Cuirassier Regiment. In 1748, it absorbed two squadrons each of the disbanded KR Ronnow and KR L'Annonciade.

The regiment capitulated to the Prussians in 1756. In 1763, a new Königlicher Prinz Cuirassier Regiment was formed and almost immediately changed its name to Kurprinz. The next year to Ronnow Cuirassier Regiment. Disbanded in 1778 when it was incorporated into the *Karabinier* Regiment.

Inhaber
1703 *Flemming*
1706 *Prinz Alexander*
1727 *Prinz Friedrich*
1733 *Kurprinz*
1734-56 *Königlicher Prinz Friedrich Christian* [80]
1763 [New] *Königlicher Prinz*
1763 *Kurprinz*
1764 *Ronnow*
1778 Disbanded

Commander
c1756 *GM Graf Ronnow*

Uniform (1740-56)
HEADWEAR: Plain black tricorn with light blue pom-pom
STOCKS: Red
COAT: White coat with light blue collar, cuffs and turnbacks. The cuffs had three white metal buttons (1740-48) and two buttons (1748-56).

---

[80] Capitulated to the Prussians in 1756

WAISTCOAT: The collarless light buff [*Lederkoller*] waistcoat that was worn on field service beneath the cuirass. In 1753, the waistcoat received a light blue collar and the lacing was changed to white-light blue-white-light blue-white.

BUTTONS: White metal

CUIRASS: Black lacquered cuirass lined with light blue cloth

LEGWEAR: Buff breeches and black long cavalry boots.

Kettledrummer of the KR2 Königlicher Prinz, 1748

KR3 Maffey / Vitzthum (1702-78)

Raised in 1702 as a Cuirassier Regiment and incorporated into the Renard Dragoon Regiment in 1778.

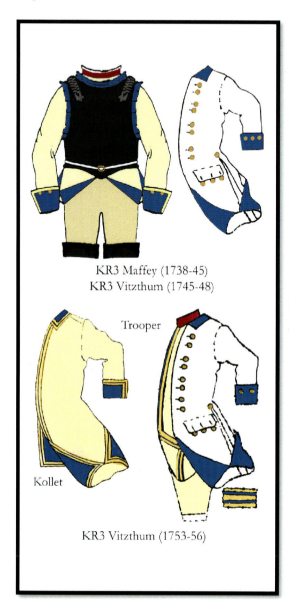

KR3 Maffey (1738-45)
KR3 Vitzthum (1745-48)

Trooper
Kollet

KR3 Vitzthum (1753-56)

Inhaber
1702 *von Tiesenhausen*
1704 *von Gersdorff*
1706 *aus dem Winckel*
1713 *Althann / Althahn*
1714 *von Kyau*
1715 *von Arnstädt*
1717 *von Pflugk*
1728 *von Hackeborn*
1730 *von Polenz*
1734 *Venediger*
1738 *Maffey*
1745-56 *GM von Vitzthum*[81]
1763 [New] *GM von Vitzthum*
1765 *Benkendorf*
1778 Disbanded

Commander
1756-63 *Oberst von Rheden*

Uniform (1740-56)
HEADWEAR: Plain black tricorn with light blue pom-pom
STOCKS: Red
FACINGS: Light blue
BUTTONS: Brass [2:2:2:2]
CUIRASS: Black lacquered cuirass line with light blue cloth
LEGWEAR: Buff breeches

---

[81] Disbanded in 1756.

Saxon Army 1740-1763

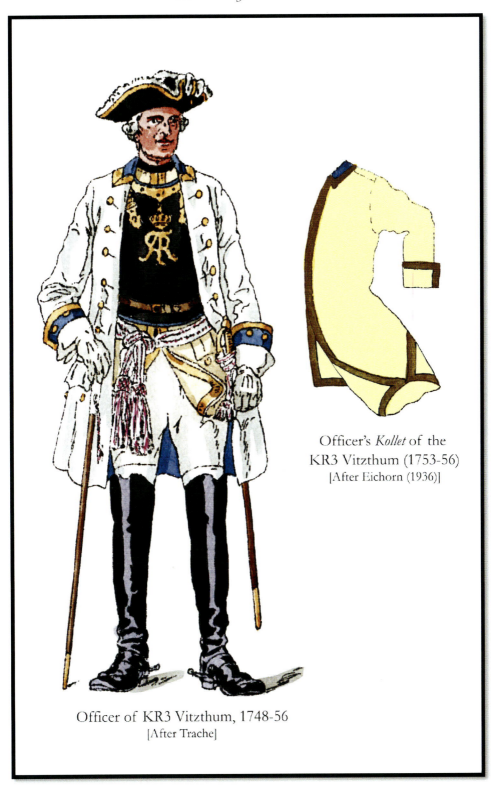

Officer's *Kollet* of the
KR3 Vitzthum (1753-56)
[After Eichorn (1936)]

Officer of KR3 Vitzthum, 1748-56
[After Trache]

Cuirassier Regiments 1732-48

"KR-iv" Haudring / Ronnow (1694-1748)

Formed in 1694. It was disbanded in 1748 with the men becoming part of KR1 *Leib-Regiment* and KR2 *Königlich Prinz* cuirassier regiments.

Inhaber
1694 *von Bunau*
1698 *Lubomirski*
1699 *von Steinau*
1706 *von Damnitz*
1713 *Johnston*
1715 *von Zuhlen*
1717 *von Criegern / Kriegern*
1735 *GM von Arnim*
1740 *von Haudring*
1746 *von Ronnow*
1748 Disbanded

Commander
c1756 *Oberst von Berlepsch*

Uniform (1740-48)
HEADWEAR: Plain black tricorn with light blue pom-pom
STOCKS: Red
FACINGS: Yellow
BUTTONS: White metal [2:2:2:2].
CUIRASS: Black lacquered cuirass line with yellow cloth
LEGWEAR: Buff breeches

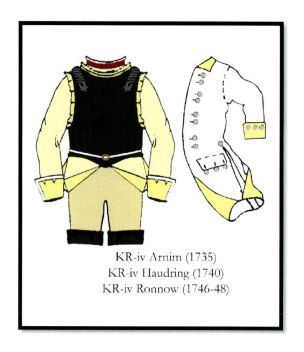

KR-iv Arnim (1735)
KR-iv Haudring (1740)
KR-iv Ronnow (1746-48)

"KR-v" Promnitz / O'Byrn (1732-48)

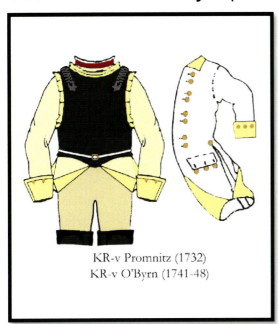

KR-v Promnitz (1732)
KR-v O'Byrn (1741-48)

Formed in 1732. It was disbanded in 1748 and became part of KR6 *Arnim*.

Inhaber
1732 *Promnitz*
1741 *Johann Jacob O'Byrn*
1748 Disbanded

Uniform (1740-48)
HEADWEAR: Plain black tricorn with light blue pom-pom
STOCKS: Red
FACINGS: Yellow
BUTTONS: Brass [2:2:2:2]
CUIRASS: Black cuirass lined with yellow cloth
LEGWEAR: Buff breeches

Kürassier vom Kürassier-Regiment O'Byrn. 1712.

"KR-vi" Nassau / Minckwitz (1731-48)

Formed in 1731 and disbanded in 1748 with the men becoming part of KR5 *von Plötz*.

Inhaber
1731 *von Nassau*
1745 *Minckwitz*
1748 Disbanded

Uniform (1740-48)
HEADWEAR: Plain black tricorn with light blue pom-pom
STOCKS: Red
FACINGS: Red
BUTTONS: Brass [2:2:2:2]
CUIRASS: Black cuirass line with red cloth
LEGWEAR: Buff breeches

KR-vi Nassau (1731)
KR-vi Minckwitz (1745-48)

"KR-vii" Brand / Mitwitz / L'Annonciade (1732-48)

It was formed in 1732 from the grenadier companies of the Dragoon regiments. Disbanded in 1748 with the men becoming part of KR1 *Leib-Regiment* and KR2 *Königlich Prinz*.

Inhaber
1732 *von Brand*
1735 *Mitwitz*
1745 *von Bestenbostel*
1746 *L'Annonciade*
1748 Disbanded

Uniform (1740-48)
HEADWEAR: Plain black tricorn with light blue pom-pom
STOCKS: Red
FACINGS: Green
BUTTONS: White metal [2:2:2:2]
CUIRASS: Black cuirass lined with green cloth
LEGWEAR: Buff breeches

KR-vii Mitwitz (1735)
KR-vii von Bestenbostel (1745)
KR-vii L'Annonciade (1746-48)

"KR-viii" Gersdorf / Dallwitz Cuirassier (1730-48)

Formed in 1730 as a *Grenadiers à Cheval* Regiment with four companies and the next year renamed *Prinz Christian* Dragoons. In 1732 augmented with an additional two companies, and in 1733 formed "KR-viii" *Sachsen-Gotha* Cuirassier regiment. It was merged in 1748 with the DR1 *Rechenberg* to form the KR6 *Rechenberg* Cuirassier Regiment.

Inhaber
Grenadiers à Cheval Regiment
1730 Sachsen Gotha
Dragoons Regiment
1731 *Prinz Christian Sachsen-Gotha*
Cuirassier Regiment
1733 *Sachsen-Gotha*
1741 *Gersdorf*
1745 *Johann Friedrich von Dallwitz*
1748 Disbanded

KR-viii Sachsen-Gotha (1733)
KR-viii Gersdorf (1741)
KR-viii Dallwitz (1745-48)

Uniform (1740-48)
HEADWEAR: Plain black tricorn with light blue pom-pom
STOCKS: Red
FACINGS: Red
BUTTONS: White metal [2:2:2:2]
CUIRASS: Black cuirass lined with red cloth
LEGWEAR: Buff breeches

Cuirassiers Regiments formed in 1748

Three cuirassier regiments were formed by converting three dragoon regiments as already explained.

KR4 Rechenberg / von Anhalt-Dessau (1748-1806)

Raised in 1698 as a Dragoon Regiment and in 1748 converted into a Cuirassier Regiment in 1748. The regiment capitulated to the Prussians in 1756. In 1763, the new Anhalt Cuirassier Regiment was reformed.

Inhaber
Dragoon Regiment - See *Rechenberg Dragoons*
Cuirassier Regiment
1748 *Rechenberg* [converted from the Dragoon Regiment]
1748 *Sondershausen*
1749-56 *Fürst Eugen von Dessau-Anhalt* [82]
1763 [New] *Fürst Eugen von Dessau-Anhalt*
1786 *Rex*
1786 *Bellegarde*
1789 *Zezschwitz*
1801 *Kochtitzky*
1809 *Zastrow* [Disbanded in 1813]

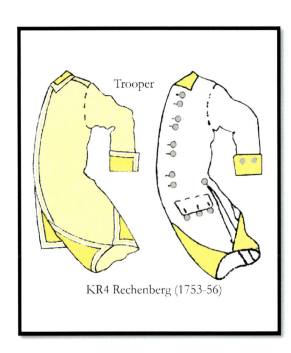

KR4 Rechenberg (1753-56)

Commander
1756-63 *Oberst von Dallwitz*

Uniform (1748-56)
HEADWEAR: Plain black tricorn with light blue pom-pom
STOCKS: Red
WAISTCOAT: The collarless light buff [*Lederkoller*] waistcoat was worn on field service beneath the cuirass.
CUFFS: Light blue cuffs edged white
TURNBACKS: White edging to the turnbacks.
BUTTONS: White metal [2:2:2:2]
CUIRASS: Black lacquered cuirass line with yellow cloth
LEGWEAR: Buff breeches

---

[82] Capitulated to the Prussians in 1756

KR5 Plötz (1748-78)

Raised in 1704 as a Dragoon Regiment and was converted to a Cuirassier Regiment in 1748. Disbanded in 1778 and incorporated into the Sacken Dragoon Regiment.

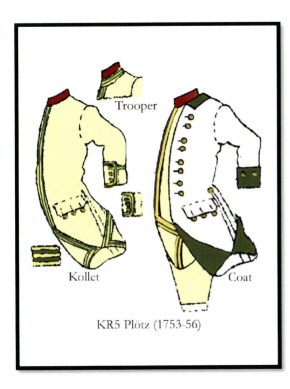

KR5 Plötz (1753-56)

Inhaber
See *DR Plötz*
Cuirassier Regiment
1748 *GL von Plötz* [Capitulated to the Prussians in 1756]
1764 [New] *Brenkendorf*
1778 Disbanded

Commander
c1756 *Oberst von Driberg*

Uniform (1740-78)
HEADWEAR: Plain black tricorn.
STOCKS: Red
FACINGS: Green
BUTTONS: Brass [2:2:2:2]
CUIRASS: Black lacquered cuirass line with green cloth
LEGWEAR: Buff breeches

KR6 von Arnim (1748-78)

KR6 von Arnim, 1748-56
[After Trache]

In 1748 converted from the Dragoon to a Cuirassier Regiment. In 1778 incorporated into the Kurfürst Cuirassier Regiment.

Inhaber
1748-56 *von Arnim*
1763 *von Arnim*
Disbanded 1778

Uniform (1748-78)
HEADWEAR: Plain black tricorn.
STOCKS: Red.
FACINGS: Crimson.
BUTTONS: Brass [2:2:2:2]
CUIRASS: Black lacquered cuirass line with green cloth.
LEGWEAR: Buff breeches.

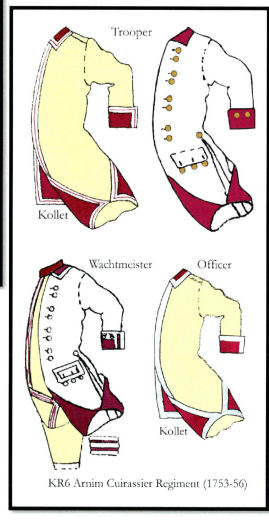

KR6 Arnim Cuirassier Regiment (1753-56)

Saxon Army 1740-1763

Officer of KR6 von Arnim, 1763
[Wilhelm von Dietrich (1907)]

Cuirassier Uniform

Uniform 1734-48

Cuirassier trooper's tricorn

Cuirassier officer's tricorn

HEADWEAR: Plain black tricorn with pom-pom in facing colour

STOCKS: Red stock for the *Leib-Regiment* otherwise black..

COAT: On 23 July 1734, the coat changed from red to white. The white coat was not used for field service. The buttons were arranged as 2:2:2:2. The cuffs were in the facing colour. A stripe of facing colour down the turnbacks

Table 15: Cuirassier Regiments 1734-48.
The facings include collar, cuffs, turnbacks and shoulder-strap.[83]

	Coat	*Kollet*	Collar, cuffs & Turnbacks	Buttons
KR1 *Leib-Cuirassier Regt.*	white	light buff [*paille*]	sky blue [*bleumourant*]	yellow
KR2 *Königlich Prinz* (1735)	white	light buff [*paille*]	sky blue [*bleumourant*]	white
KR3 *von Vendiger* (1735) *Maffey* (1748) *von Vitzthum* (1745)	white	light buff [*paille*]	light blue [*hellblau*] then dark blue [*dunkelblau*] (1737)	yellow
"KR-iv" *von Arnim* (1735) *von Handung* (1745) *von Ronnow* (1746)	white	light buff [*paille*]	lemon yellow [*zitr. gelb*]	white
"KR-v" *von Promnitz* (1732) *von O'Byrn* (1741)	white	light buff [*paille*]	yellow [*gelb*]	yellow
"KR-vi" *Prinz Nassau* (1731) *Minkwitz* (1745)	white	light buff [*paille*]	red [*rot*] [84]	yellow
"KR-vii" *Mitchau* (1735) *Bestenhostel* (1745) *L'Annonciade* (1746)	white	light buff [*paille*]	green [*grün*]	white
"KR-viii" *Sachsen Gotha* *Senssdorff* (1745) *Dalhwitz* (1746)	white	light red [*hellrot*] then *paille* (1746)	light red [*hellrot*] then white (1744)	white

---

[83] Friedrich (1998) 20
[84] Until 1740 light red [*Hellrot*]. [Friedrich (1998) 20] Changed to crimson in 1745.

Saxon Army 1740-1763

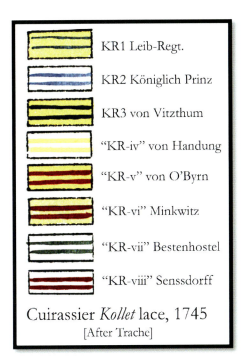

Cuirassier *Kollet* lace, 1745
[After Trache]

- KR1 Leib-Regt.
- KR2 Königlich Prinz
- KR3 von Vitzthum
- "KR-iv" von Handung
- "KR-v" von O'Byrn
- "KR-vi" Minkwitz
- "KR-vii" Bestenhostel
- "KR-viii" Senssdorff

WAISTCOAT: The collarless light buff [*Lederkoller*] waistcoat with cuffs and stripe down the turnbacks in the facing colour was worn on field service beneath the cuirass. Until 1746 the *Kollet was* light red [*hellrot*] before it became *paille*.

CUIRASS: Black lacquered cuirass with no back plate lined with cloth in the facing colour that projected out from beneath at the neck, shoulders and waist.

LEGWEAR: Buff breeches and long black cavalry boots.

EQUIPMENT: A buff belt over the left shoulder supporting a buff cartridge box and carbine swivel. The sword was carried in a scabbard

DISTINCTIONS: Officer's *Kollet* and waistcoats had gold or silver lace according to button colour. White-crimson sash. The cuirass had the "*AR*" cipher.

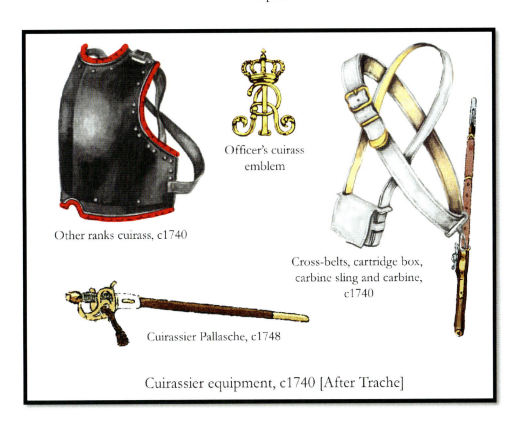

Other ranks cuirass, c1740

Officer's cuirass emblem

Cross-belts, cartridge box, carbine sling and carbine, c1740

Cuirassier Pallasche, c1748

Cuirassier equipment, c1740 [After Trache]

Uniform 1748-56

HEADWEAR: Black tricorn with white cockade. Officers and NCO tricorn had edging in button colour.
STOCK: Black.
COAT: White coat with collar, cuffs and turnbacks in facing colour. Button arranged 1, 2 and 3, under it on the right in the coat edge were three buttons with three buttonholes. There were three buttons on the coat pockets and cuffs. Another two on the back.
WAISTCOAT: *Paille* (light yellow) *Kollet* sleeved waistcoat with lace edgings in the facing colour.
STABLE CLOTHING: Stable smocks were made of sail canvas and white field caps with facing colour on forehead and tassel.

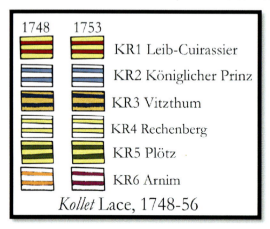

Table 16: Cuirassier Regiments 1748-56.
White lapels and breeches in the facing colour. Light buff [*paille*] *Kollet*.[85]

	Coat	Collar, cuffs & Turnbacks	Buttons
KR1 *Leib Regt.*	white	red [*rot*]	brass
KR2 *Königlich Prinz*	white	sky blue [*bleumourant*]	white metal
KR3 *von Vitzthum*	white	dark blue [*dunkelblau*]	brass
KR4 *von Rechenberg*	white	yellow [*gelb*]	white metal
KR5 *von Plötz*	white	green [*grün*]	white metal
KR6 *von Arnim*	white	orange[86]	white metal

---

[85] Friedrich (1998) 23
[86] The facings changed to crimson in 1753.

Saxon Army 1740-1763

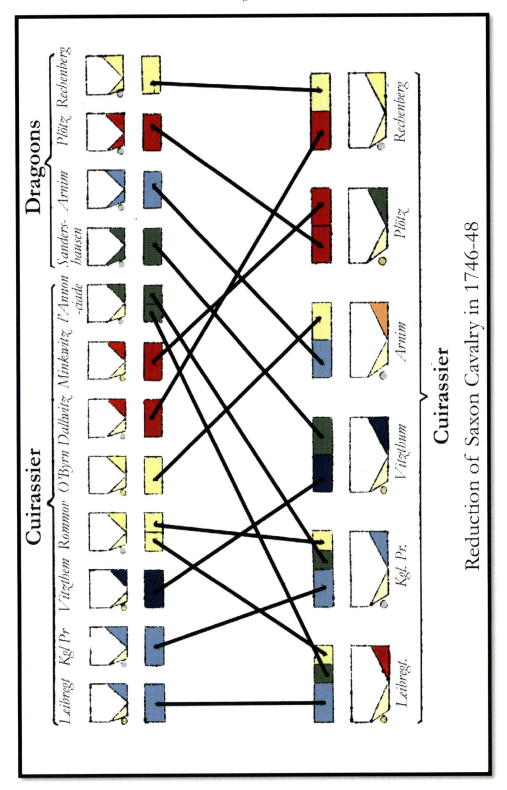

DISTINCTIONS: Officer's *Kollet* and waistcoats had gold or silver lace according to button colour. White-crimson sash.

HORSE FURNITURE: Saddlecloths and holster covers were in facing colours with white edge and two stripes in facing colour. Officer's had a gold or silver edging according to button colour.

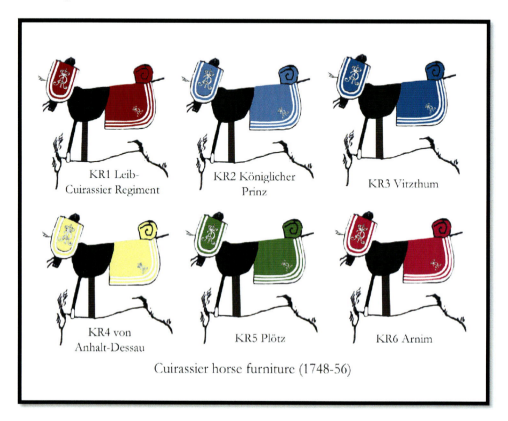

Cuirassier horse furniture (1748-56)

Trumpeters and Kettledrummers
These wore reversed colours.

COAT: White coat with turnbacks in the facing colour.

LACE: Braid in the button colour with facing colour running through it.

EQUIPMENT: The *Leib-Regiment* had silver trumpets and brass for the other Regiments. Kettledrum hangings were in facing colour with gold or silver embroidery.

Saxon Army 1740-1763

Trumpeters of the KR5 Plötz
[After Trache and Dietrich]

Chapter 9:
Saxon Dragoons

In 1730, the Saxon Army had four Dragoon Regiments. Each regiment had three squadrons of two companies plus a grenadier company made up of three officers and 2 drummers plus a detachment of one corporal and 10 dragoons.[87]

Regimental staff (16 men)
1 *Oberst*, 1 *Oberst-Lt*, 1 Major, 1 *Regiments-Quartiermeister*, 1 *Adjutant*,
1 *Auditeur*, 1 *Regiments-Feldscher* [regimental surgeon], 1 kettledrummer,
1 provost, 1 servant, 6 *Hautboisten* [musicians].

Six Companies (6 coys of 90 men = 560 men)
4 captains, 2 staff-captain, 6 first lieutenant, 6 second lieutenants,
6 *Fähnrich*, 12 *Wachtmeister*, 6 *Fahnen-Junker*, 6 *Fourier*, 6 *Feldscher*
[surgeon], 24 corporals, 12 drummers, 480 dragoons.

In 1732 the grenadier company from the Dragoon regiments was used to for "KR-iv" *von Brand*. Every dragoon regiment had now 6 companies formed into three, later two squadrons with a total of 469 men.

Regimental staff (19 men)
1 *Oberst*, 1 *Oberst-Lt*, 1 major, 1 *Regiments-Quartiermeister*, 1 Adjutant,
1 *Auditeur*, 1 *Prediger*, 1 *Regiments-Feldscher*, 1 kettledrummer, 1 provost, 1
servant, 8 *Hautboisten* [musicians].

Six Companies (6 coys of 75 men = 450 men):
4 captains, 2 staff-captains, 6 first lieutenants, 6 second lieutenants,
6 *Fähnrich*, 12 *Wachtmeister*, 6 *Fahnen-Junker*, 6 *Feldscher*, 24 *Korporale*,
12 *Tamboure*, 6 *Fourier*, 360 Dragoons.

Dragoon regiments were disbanded in 1748 and the men transferred to the Cuirassier regiments. [See Chapter 8]

---

[87] Hasse & Eichhorn (1936) 9.

DR1 von Rechenberg

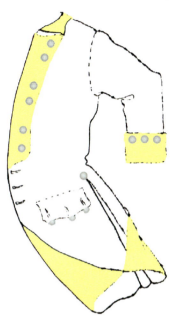

DR1 von Rechenberg
1741-48

Formed as a Dragoon regiment in 1698 and was converted into KR6 Rechenberg when it absorbed the disbanded "KR-viii" Dallwitz.

Inhaber
1698 *Wolfenbüttel*
1701 *Milkau*
1717 *von Birkholtz*
1726 *von Arnstädt I*
1732 *von Arnstädt II*
1741 *von Rechenberg*
1748 Became KR *Rechenberg*

Uniform
FACINGS: Yellow
BUTTONS: White metal [2:2:2]

DR2 von Sondershausen-Schwarzburg

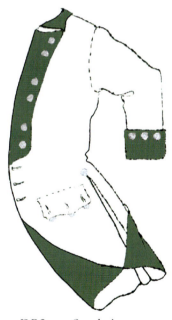

DR2 von Sonderhausen-Schwartzburg, 1742-48

In 1748, the regiment was converted into the KR3 von Vitzthum.

Inhaber
1700 *von Goltz*
1712 *von Flemming*
1715 *von Bielke*
1719 *von Diemar*
1719 *von Sitzen*
1724 *von Weissenbach*
1724 *von Katte*
1733 *von Leipziger*
1742 *von Sondershausen-Schwarzburg*
1748 Disbanded and became KR *Vitzthum*

Uniform
FACINGS: Green
BUTTONS: White metal [2:2:2]

DR3 von Schlichting

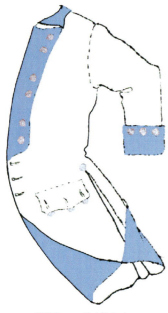

DR3 von Schlichting
1741-42

In 1748, it was converted into the KR4 von Arnim Cuirassier Regiment.

Inhaber
1703 *Oertzen*
1705 *Dunewald*
1711 *Sachsen-Weissenfels*
1717 *Unruh*
1728 *von Goldacker*
1734 *von Schlichting*
1745 *von Arnim*
1748 Became the *KR Arnim*

Uniform
FACINGS: Sky blue [*Bleumourant*]
BUTTONS: White metal [2:2:2]

DR4 von Plötz

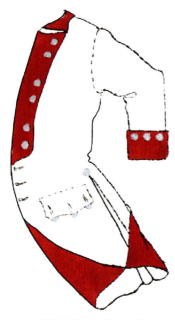

DR4 Plötz, 1741-42

In 1704, it was formed as the Wrangel Dragoons and in 1748 converted into the KR5 von Plötz Cuirassier Regiment.

Inhaber
1704 *Wrangel Dragoons*
1710 *Baudissin*
1717 *Klingenberg*
1729 *Chevalier George de Saxe*
1741 von *Pirch*
1744 von *Plötz*
1748 Became *KR Plötz*

Uniform
FACINGS: Light red
BUTTONS: White metal [2:2:2]

Saxon Army 1740-1763

Dragoon Corporal of DR4 Pirsch, 1741
[Wilhelm Dietricxh, 1907]

Dragoon Uniforms
Dragoon Uniform (1735-41)
On 23 July 1734, Dragoons received white skirts instead of red.

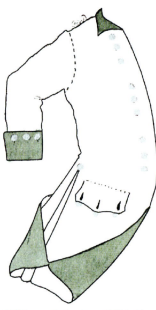

COAT: Single-breasted white coat with the buttons on the right side and buttonholes on the left coat side.

LAPELS: No lapels.

BUTTONS: These were arranged 2:2:2, with the exception of the DR von Leipzig (1737 Prinz Schwarzburg-Sangerhausen) that had the buttons in the arrangement from 3:3:3. Staff officers had coat buttons equally spaced.

WAISTCOAT: *Paille* [light buff] waistcoat. Officers wore waistcoats in facing colour.

LEGWEAR: *Paille* [light buff] breeches.

SIDEARMS: Officers and NCOs were also armed with muskets with bayonets.

DR2 von Leipziger, 1734-41
[After Trache]

Kettledrummer
Each kettledrummer had a pair of kettledrums with hangings in facing colour and decorated in silver embroidery. None were lost until the dragoons were disbanded. It is not confirmed that DR2 von Katte received yellow hangings for their kettledrums in 1733.[88]

Table 17: Dragoon kettledrum hangings.[89]

	Hangings	Decorations
DR1 *von Arnstädt*	dark blue [*dunkelblau*]	silver
DR2 *von Leipziger*	parrot green [*papageigrün*]	silver
DR3 *Goldacker*	grass green [*grasgrün*]	silver
DR4 *Chevalier de Saxe*	sky blue [*bleumourant*]	silver

Drummers
In 1730 each regiment had twelve copper drums. These were replaced by brass drums in 1735.

---

[88] Hasse & Eichhorn (1936) 9
[89] Hasse & Eichhorn (1936) 10

Saxon Army 1740-1763

Drummer of DR1 von Rechenberg, 1741-48
[Wilhelm von Dietrich, 1907]

Dragoon Uniform (1741-48)

On 18 April 1741, the coat was instructed to have lapels in the facing colour.

HEADWEAR: Tricorn with silver edging.
COAT: Double-breasted white coat with collar, cuffs, lapels and turnbacks in facing colours was introduced.
LAPELS: In facing colour.
BUTTONS: The buttons (2:2:2).
LEGWEAR: Buff coloured breeches.
SIDEARMS: Officers and NCOs were also armed with muskets with bayonets.

Table 18: Saxon Dragoon Regiments in 1735-48.

Regiment	Coat	Facings	Buttons	Saddlecloth
DR1 *von Arnstädt* (1732) *von Rechenberg* (1741) Disbanded 1748	white	Yellow [*hellgelb*]	white	Red with plain white border lines
DR2 *Leipziger* (1733) *von Schwarzburg* (1742) Disbanded 1748	white	light green [*papageigrün*] or apple green	white	Red
DR3 *von Schlichting* (1734) *von Arnim* (1745) Disbanded 1748	white	sky blue [*bleumourant*] [90]	white	Red
DR4 *Chevalier de Saxe* (1729) *von Pirch* (1741) *von Plötz* (1744) Disbanded 1748	white	light red [*hellrot*] [91]	white	Scarlet with plain white border lines

---

[90] Manley (1998) confused the change in facings of crimson with the new KR Arnim that was formed in 1748.
[91] Manley (1998) confused the change in facings of green with the new KR Plötz that was formed in 1748.

Chapter 10: Chevauleger

In 1733, the *Chevauleger* were raised in Poland to provide western style cavalry using the smaller Polish horses that had previously been classed as "unmilitary." These horses were mostly coppery-red chestnut (sorrels) in lighter shades with the manes and tails in the same colour. From 1753, each regiment had eight companies in four squadrons with 762 dragoons.

At Leuthen (5 Dec 1756), the three Saxon *Chevauleger* Regiments amounted to about 1,200 men as part of the cavalry vanguard detached at Borne under Marshal Nostitz that were driven back on the Austrian right wing by the Prussian vanguard. They were transferred to the left flank where they were thrown against the main Prussian flank attack that routed the Austrian and Allied army. The *Chevauleger* lost 479 men killed wounded or captured.

CL1 Prinz Karl Chevauleger

Raised in 1733 as two companies of dragoons and two companies of *Jäger zu Pferde* serving in Poland. On 6 November 1735, it was augmented to four squadrons under the name of *Prinz Karl Chevauleger* Regiment.

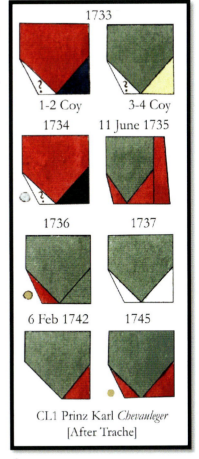

CL1 Prinz Karl *Chevauleger*
[After Trache]

Inhaber
Chevauleger
1733 *Prinz Karl von Sachsen*
1758 *Herzog von Kurland*
1796 *Dehn-Rothfelser*
1799-1811 *Prinz Clemens*

Commanders
1745-1757 *Oberst-Lt Nostitz* [92]
1757-1765 *Oberst von Benkendorf* [93]

Uniform (1733)
HEADWEAR: Black tricorn.
COAT: The I & II companies were uniformed as dragoons with a red coat, deep-blue facings and brass buttons. The III & IV companies were uniformed as Jäger with a green coat with yellow facings and brass buttons. In 1734, all the

---

[92] 1757 GL and mortally wounded during the battle of Leuthen.
[93] 1761 GM

Uniform (1734-47)
COAT: The coat for all four companies was red, black facings and brass buttons.
LEGWEAR: Red breeches and long black boots.
SADDLECLOTH: The saddlecloth was red.

Uniform (1738-63)
HEADWEAR: Black tricorn with yellow lace and red pompom.
STOCK: Red.
COAT: Parrot green coat [*papageigrün*].

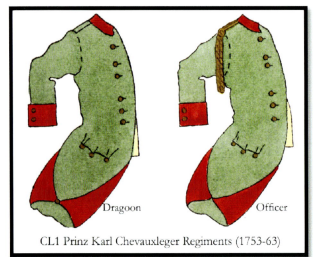

CL1 Prinz Karl Chevauxleger Regiments (1753-63)

FACINGS: Red.
LAPELS: None.
SHOULDER KNOTS: Yellow aiguillette with yellow metal tassel.
WAISTCOAT: Red and changed to straw in 1753.
BUTTONS: Brass [1:2:3].
LEGWEAR: Straw or white breeches and black cavalry boots.
SIDEARMS: A sword, a pair of pistols and a musket.
SADDLECLOTH: Parrot green with yellow border plus cipher and crown.
SABRETACHE: Green bordered with a yellow braid ornamented with two red stripes.

Musician Uniform
COAT: Red.
COLLAR & CUFFS: Green.
TURNBACKS: Green.
WAISTCOAT: Green.
BUTTONS: Brass [arranged 1:2:3].
LACE: Red-yellow-red lace swallow's nest, sleeve, cuffs, pocket and breast.
EQUIPMENT: Trumpet had green-red-yellow lace. Drums had green-red striped border. The silver kettledrum had red-gold hangings.

Saxon Army 1740-1763

CL1 Prinz Karl von Sachsen Chevauleger Regiment, 1748-63
[After Trache]

Campaign History

War of the Polish Succession: The regiment took part in the campaign in Poland against the "Confederates" (1734-35).

War of the Austrian Succession: The regiment took part in the campaigns of 1742, 1744-45 in Bohemia and Saxony.

Seven Years War: In 1756, during the invasion of Saxony by the Prussians, the regiment was stationed in Poland when much of the Saxon army surrendered at Pirna.

From 1757, the regiment served with the Austrian army. It fought at Kolin (18 June) where they broke the Prussian Cavalry of General Hülsen and threw his infantry into confusion permitting the Austrian infantry to rally. The Austrians captured 14 Prussian battalions along with all of their guns. The regiment was then present at Moys (7 Sept) and Breslau (22 Nov). The regiment took part in the victorious battle of Breslau where it was deployed in the first line of the cavalry left wing of *Nádasdy Corps*. At Leuthen (5 Dec), their commander *Oberst-Lt Nostitz* who according to Duffy[94] was "a first class officer" was mortally wounded. Prinz Karl Chevauleger lost 214 dragoons, more than half of the regiment.

In June and July 1758 the regiment particularly distinguished itself at the relief of Olmütz when a large Prussian convoy was destroyed forcing Frederick II to abandon the siege with heavy losses. On 29 October 1762, the regiment took part in the battle of Freiberg.

---

[94] Duffy, *Prussia's Glory*

CL2 Graf Brühl Chevauleger

Raised 1733 by *Oberst Sybilski* of 2 squadrons using drafts from the whole army. In 1735 it was augmented to four squadrons of two companies each and now entitled CL2 *Sybilski Chevauleger*. In 1756 the regiment had eight companies in four squadrons with a total of 762 men.

Inhaber
1734 *Sybilski, Frhr. von Wolfsberg*
1748 *HeinrichGraf von Brühl*[95]
1764 *LG Renard* [resigned 1778]
1779 *Goldacker*
1788 *Weimar*
1793 *Rössler*
1801 *Polenz*
1812 Destroyed in Russia

Commanders
1753 *Oberst von Gössnitz* [d. 1763]
1758 *Oberst Friedrich Graf Brühl*
1763 *Oberst von Diepow* [d. 1771]

Dragoon Uniform
HEADWEAR: Sky blue cloth high fronted had with royal cipher and crown.
STOCK: Red.
COAT: Grey coat
COLLAR & CUFFS: Sky blue.
TURNBACKS: Sky blue.
LAPELS: Sky blue.
SHOULDER KNOTS: White with white metal tassel.
WAISTCOAT: Sky blue.
BUTTONS: Brass [arranged 1:2:3].
LEGWEAR: Straw or white breeches and black cavalry boots.
HORSE FURNITURE: Sky blue with white-red-white-red-white border, cipher and crown in white.

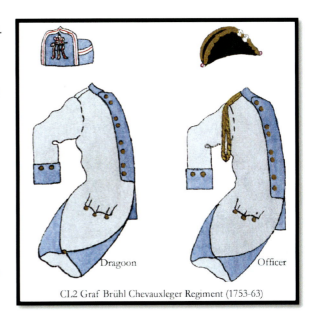
CL2 Graf Brühl Chevauxleger Regiment (1753-63)

---

[95] Died 1763

Musician
Kettledrummers rode brown piebald horses.
COAT: Grey coat.
COLLAR, CUFFS and TURNBACKS: Sky blue.
WAISTCOAT: Sky blue.
BUTTONS: Brass.
LACE: Drummers had sky blue-yellow-sky blue lace on swallow's nest, sleeve, cuffs, pocket and breast.
LEGWEAR: Straw breeches and black cavalry boots.
EQUIPMENT: Trumpet with Red-White lace. Drum had red border. The brass kettledrum had sky blue hangings.

Campaign History
War of Polish Succession: The regiment was sent immediately to Poland. Along with the *Jäger zu Pferd* of Oberst Vitzthum von Eckstädt, they engaged in numerous actions in greater Poland during the siege of Danzig.

War of Austrian Succession: Participated in the campaigns of 1742, 1744-45. On 13 December 1745 it charged the Prussian rearguard along with some Ulan near Lommatsch and Zehren and captured three standards and two pairs of silver kettledrums. The commanding enemy General von Röhl was killed. At Kolin, it cut into the Prussian infantry and took nine colours.

Seven Years War: In 1756, the regiment was stationed in Poland so avoided the fate of the Saxon Army captured at Pirna. In 1757, the regiment served with the Austrian army. At Kolin (18 June) the Saxon Chevauleger along with the Austrian Ligne Dragoons fell on the right flank on the exposed Prussian corps. They broke Hülsen's cavalry and threw his infantry into confusion. Wied's infantry division rallied and the Austrian and Saxon cavalry attacked again. Hülsen's infantry were broken and formed squares. After a short fight, the Austrians captured 14 Prussian battalions along with all their guns. At Moys (7 Sept), the regiment was deployed in the second line of the right wing under GM Gosenitz. The regiment fought at Breslau (22 Nov) and at Leuthen (5 Dec), the regiment was part of the cavalry vanguard under Nostitz which was attacked and driven back on the Austrian right wing by the Prussian vanguard.

Saxon Army 1740-1763

CL2 Graf Brühl Chevauleger Regiment, 1748-63
[After Trache]

CL3 Prinz Albrecht Chevauleger

Raised 1745 in the Marienburg area of Poland around the Marienburg Castle of the Teutonic Order by Oberst von Wilmsdorf and operated along the Silesian border. In 1756 this regiment had eight companies in four squadrons with a total of 762 Dragoons.

Inhaber
1745-1812 *LG Herzog Albrecht of Saxony and Poland, Duke of Saxe-Teschen.*

Commander
1754 *GM von Monroe*
1759 GM *Graf Renard*[96]
1812 Destroyed in Russia

CL3 Prinz Albrecht *Chevauleger* Regiment, 1745-53

Uniform 1745-53
HEADWEAR: Black tricorn with yellow lace
STOCK: Red
COAT: Grey coat
COLLAR, CUFFS and TURNBACKS: Black
LAPELS: Black
SHOULDER KNOTS: White with yellow metal tassel
WAISTCOAT: Buff
BUTTONS: White metal

---

[96] Received his own regiment in 1764.

LEGWEAR: Straw or white breeches and black heavy cavalry boots

HORSE FURNITURE: Grey with white-yellow-white-yellow-white border, cipher and crown in white.

Trumpeter, standard bearer and drummer of the CL3 Prinz Albrecht Chevauxleger, 1745-53

Musician

COAT: Green coat with white collar, cuffs and turnbacks.

WAISTCOAT: White

BUTTONS: White metal

LACE: Drummers had yellow-white-yellow on swallow nest, sleeve, cuffs, pocket and breast

LEGWEAR: Straw breeches and black cavalry boots

EQUIPMENT: Trumpet with Green-yellow-white lace. Drums had red-white striped border. Silver kettledrums with red and silver hangings.

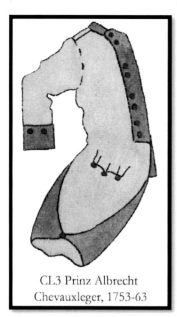

CL3 Prinz Albrecht Chevauxleger, 1753-63

Uniform 1745-53
HEADWEAR: Black tricorn with yellow lace
STOCK: Red
COAT: Grey coat
COLLAR, CUFFS and TURNBACKS: Green
LAPELS: Green
WAISTCOAT: Green.
BUTTONS: Brass
LEGWEAR: Straw or white breeches and black heavy cavalry boots
HORSE FURNITURE: Green with white-red-white-red-white border, and white cipher and crown.

Campaign History
Seven Years War. In 1756, the regiment was stationed in Poland so avoided the fate of the Saxon units captured at Pirna. In 1757, the regiment served with the Austrian army. At Kolin (18 June), the Saxon *Chevauleger* with the struck the right flank of the exposed Prussians of Hülsen and Tresckow. This allowed the Austrian infantry to rally. The Austrians captured fourteen Prussian battalions along with all their guns. It fought at Breslau (22 Nov) and Leuthen (5 Dec) where the regiment was part of the cavalry vanguard under Nostitz and driven back on the Austrian right wing by the Prussian vanguard.

Saxon Army 1740-1763

CL4 Graf Rutowski Chevauleger

The regiment was raised 1742 in Saxony by Oberst Vitzthum von Eckstädt. In 1756 this regiment formed 8 coys in 4 squadrons with a total of 514 men book strength. In October 1756 it was captured at Pirna and the men incorporated into the second Bn of the Prussian Dragoon Regiment DR12 Herzog von Württemberg Dragoons. In 1763 the regiment reformed with four squadrons and incorporated the Hussar Squadron von Schill.

CL4 Graf Rutowsky Chevauxleger, 1753-63

Inhaber
Chevauleger
1742 *Friedrich August Graf Rutowski*
1756 Disbanded
1763 *Friedrich August Graf Rutowski*
1771 *Frhr. von Sacken*
Dragoons
1778 *Frhr. von Sacken*
Chevauleger
1784 *Frhr. von Sacken* [d. 1789]
1790 *Gersdorff*
1804 *Prinz Johann*

Commander
1745 Oberst Frhr. von Dyherrn[97]
1759 Oberst von Schlieben[98]

Dragoon Uniform (1753-56)
HEADWEAR: Black tricorn with yellow lace and red-black small pompom.
STOCK: Red.
COAT: Red coat.
FACINGS: Back.
SHOULDER KNOTS: White with yellow metal tassel
WAISTCOAT: Dark straw.
BUTTONS: White metal.
LEGWEAR: Straw or white breeches and black heavy cavalry boots
HORSE FURNITURE: Red with white-black-white-black-white border, cipher and crown in white.

---

[97] Later *General-Lieutenant* and died 1759 from the wounds suffered at the battle of Bergen.
[98] Promoted *General-Major* in 1761 and became commander of the newly raised *Reuter Regiment*. Killed 1762 in the 2nd Battle of Lutterberg.

Musician

COAT: Black coat
COLLAR, CUFFS & TURNBACKS: Red.
WAISTCOAT: Black.
BUTTONS: White metal.
LACE: Drummers had black-red-black on swallow nest, sleeve, cuffs, pocket and breast
LEGWEAR: Straw breeches and black cavalry boots
EQUIPMENT: Trumpet had black-red-yellow. Drums had red-white striped Borders. The brass kettledrums had black-silver hangings.

Campaign History

War of Austrian Succession: It served in the campaigns of 1744 and 1745 in Saxony.

Seven Years War: At the end of August 1756, when Frederick II invaded Saxony, the regiment retired to Pirna with the rest of the Saxon army. At Pirna, the regiment was deployed on the right wing under von Arnim, as part of von Rechenberg's Brigade. It surrendered with the rest of the army on 15 October. The other ranks were incorporated into the second battalion of the Prussian *DR12 Dragoon Regiment Prinz von Württemberg*. These were soon disbanded on April 1757.[99]

Two bodies, under the Sergeants Ehring and Heysing, a third under Corporal Eichler, escaped Prussian service. In Moravia, the men were distributed among the *Chevauleger* Regiments. Both Sergeants were made captains, and corporal Eichler was promoted Kornet in 1761.

CL4 Graf Rutowsky
1748

---

[99] Bleckwenn (1987) IV: 73

Chevauleger Uniform
Uniform 1735-52
HEADWEAR: Dragoons wore tricorns and the grenadier company wore grenadier's caps.
COAT: Single breasted coat that changed to a double breasted coat with lapels in facing colour in 1742.
LEGWEAR: The trousers of the *Chevauleger* and Dragoons were at this time *paille* in colour with the exception of the CL1 Prince Carl that wore red trousers.
SADDLECLOTH: The saddlecloth was in coat colour with two lines of yellow for all except CL2 Sybilski that was white.

Table 19: Saxon Chevauleger Regiments in 1735-41.

Regiment	Coat	Facings	Waistcoat	Legwear	Buttons
CL1 *Prinz Carl*	parrot green [*p. grün*]	red [*rot*]	light buff [*paille*]	red	yellow
CL2 *Sybilski*	grey [*grau*]	sky blue [*bleumourant*]	sky blue [*bleumourant*]	*paille*	white

Table 20: Saxon Chevauleger Regiments in 1742-52.

Regiment	Coat	Facings	Waistcoat	Buttons	Saddlecloth
CL1 *Prinz Carl*	green [*z. grün*]	red [*rot*] without lapels	light buff [*paille*]	yellow	green with yellow border lines
CL2 *Graf Brühl*	grey [*grau*]	sky blue [*bleumourant*]	sky blue [*bleumourant*]	yellow	light blue with plain white border lines
CL3 *Rutowski*	dark red [*dunkelrot*]	black [*schwarz*]	light buff [*paille*]	yellow	scarlet with yellow border lines
CL4 *Prinz Albrecht*	grey [*grau*]	black [*schwarz*]	dark green [*dunkelgrün*]	yellow	black with yellow border lines

Table 21: Saxon Chevauleger Regiments in 1753-63

Regiment	Coat	Facings	Waistcoat	Buttons
CL1 *Prinz Carl Chevauleger*	parrot green [*p. grün*]	red [*rot*] without lapels	Light buff [*paille*]	yellow
CL2 *Graf Brühl*	grey [*grau*]	sky blue [*bleumourant*]	sky blue [*bleumourant*]	yellow
CL3 *Graf Rutowski*	dark red [*dunkelrot*]	black [*schwarz*]	light buff [*paille*]	yellow
CL4 *Prinz Albrecht*	grey [*grau*]	green [*grün*]	dark green [*dunkelgrün*]	yellow

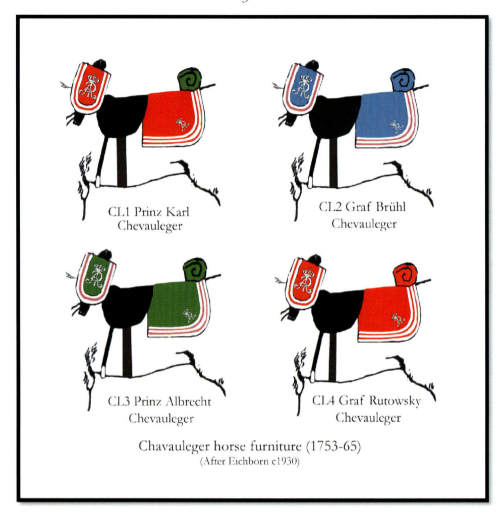

Chapter 11:
Polish Ulan Pulks

Green Ulan Pulk, 1745

The *Ulan* were maintained by the Polish Commonwealth and were hired into Saxon service. They were recruited in Lithuania and from Tartars. During peacetime, they secured the roads between Saxony and Warsaw with the regular Saxon *Chevauleger* Regiments. They were expert in the *Kleine Kreig* [Literally means little wars] where they were employed for patrol, reconnaissance, courier duty and skirmish in support of Saxon *Chevauleger*.

During the war of Polish Succession 1733-35, the *Ulan* remained loyal to the Wettin dynasty in contrast to the most of Polish-Lithuanian army. During the campaign of 1734, two Polish light horse companies acted with *Chevauleger* under Oberst-Lt Graf Bitum.[100] After the end of hostilities in 1735, the number of *Ulan* companies was increased. By 1740 the Saxon army had an *Ulan Pulk* [regiment in Polish] of twelve *Hof-Fahnen* [literally banners] commanded by Oberst von Bledowsky.[101] Further *Hof-Fahnen* were formed on 1 January (13th) and 1 May 1741 (14th and 15th).[102] These operated together under common command of Oberst Bledowsky [also spelt *Blentowski* and *Belwedowski*].[103]

---

[100] These later became the Prinz Karl *Chevauleger* [Schuster and Francke (1885)]
[101] Schuster & Francke (1885): Tessin G. (1986): Gromoboy (2009) "Polish Ulan (1730-63)."
[102] Schuster & Francke (1885); Gromoboy (2009) "Polish Ulan (1730-1763)."
[103] Tessin shows them in 1740-42 as a single regiment [Tessin (1986)]

In 1740 each *Hof-Fahne* of 71 men had
3 officers, 34 *Towarczys* [Polish nobles] and 34 *Pocztowi* [servants]..5

In autumn 1741 each *Hof-Fahne* of 100 men had
1 *Rittmeister*, 1 lieutenant, 1 *Fähnrich*, 1 kettledrummer, 46 *Towarczys* [Polish nobles] and 46 *Pocztowi* [servants].

Ulan operated with Saxon army during the First Silesian War and in March 1743 they returned to Poland where their number was increased to a total of 23 *Hof-Fahnen*[104] and reorganized into three *Pulk* of Oberst Bledowsky, Oberst Sychodzinsky and Oberst Wilczewsky [or *Wilozewsky*].

Red Ulan Pulk, 1745

---

[104] Schuster & Francke (1885); Gromoboy (2009) "Polish Ulan (1730-1763)."

At the end of September 1744 the three *Ulan Pulks* (Wilczewsky, Bledowsky and Sychodzinsky) departed for Saxony from Poland. On 2 October 1744 they joined the Main Army at Adorf. They were joined by a new *Ulan Pulk* in February 1745.

The Ulan Pulk in 1745-48 had 698 men:[105]
  1 *Oberst*, 1 *Regiments-Feldscher*, 1 kettledrummer, 7 *Rittmeister*,
  8 lieutenants, 8 cornets, 325 *Towarczys*, 8 trumpeters, 339 *Poczrowy*.

On 17 May 1745 the four *Ulan Pulks* entered Silesia with the Austro-Saxon Army.[106] These fought at Kesselsdorf (15 Dec 1745) under command of von Sybilski.[107] They returned to Poland in the middle of January 1746 and three *Ulan Pulks* were disbanded in 1748.[108] On 1 June 1754, there were the Red (*Wilczewsky*), the Blue (*Rudnicki*) and the Yellow (*Bronikowsky*) *Ulan Pulk*.[109]

---

[105] Hasse & Eichhorn (1936) 11
[106] Bertuszewsky *Pulk* had six *Hoffahnen*. The Rudnicki, *Ulan* and Boreslav [Belwedowski] *Pulks* each had eight *Hof-Fahnen*.
[107] Schuster & Francke (1885); Gromoboy (2009) "Polish Ulan (1730-1763)."
[108] Tessin (1986)
[109] Schuster & Francke (1885); Gromoboy (2009) "Polish Ulan (1730-1763)."

In March 1757, the *Red*, *Blue* and *Yellow Ulan Pulk* remained in Warsaw so did not participate in the Pirna campaign. Each Pulk had 6 *Hof-Fahnen* [banners] of 75 men. The *Red (Renard)* and *Blue (Rudnicki) Ulan Pulk* had 603 and 602 men respectively and 575 horses each joined the Saxon army forming in Hungary.[110] The *Yellow (Wilzewsky) Ulan Pulk* remained in Poland throughout war and did not participated in any actions. The Blue and Red *Ulan* operated with the Austrian army and then with the *Reichsarmee* mainly in scouting, raiding and skirmishing roles.

Blue Ulan Pulk (1749-63)

---

[110] Schuster & Francke (1885)

In 1758, they were part of FM Daun's army at the relief of the siege of Olmutz. On 17 June near Gross-Wisternitz, Graf Stainville commanding *Blue* and *Red Ulan* plus the Austrian cavalry of the Lowenstein *Chevauleger* and Dessewffy Hussars surprised eight squadrons of Bayreuth Dragoons who lost ten officers and 458 men.[111]

In 1760, both *Ulan Pulk* were part of Lacy Corps. On the night of 20 July during the relief of Dresden *Blue (Rudnicki) Ulan Pulk* together with the Esterhazy Hussars under Brentano evicted the Möhring Hussars from Leuben and drove them briskly towards Frederick II's headquarters on Grüne Wiese. The guards fled and the king in his nightshirt stood in the courtyard and shouted, "Save me! Hide me somewhere." The Prussians gathered their wits and the attackers retired in good order.[112]

On 28 September 1760, *FM Lacy* detached the reliable *GFWM Brentano* with the Esterhazy Hussars and both Polish *Ulan Pulks* to ward against interference from Frederick. The *Ulan*, upon entering Prussian territory, ravaged the area mercilessly despite attempts to restrain them. *Lacy* joined his advance guard with four regiments of horse bringing the strength to forty-three squadrons and reached Berlin on the morning of 7 October. On 10 October, the *Ulan* wrecked the Potsdam small arms factory followed by sacking the royal palace of Charlottenberg to the west of Berlin.[113]

At the battle of Torgau they were on outpost duty south of the city. In 1761, the Blue and Red *Pulk* were with Hadik Corps in FM Daun's army in Saxony, and in 1762 transferred to Maguire Corps in Saxony. In 1763, the successor to King August III of Poland, Frederick August, was unsuccessful in retaining the Polish Crown and shortly after the *Ulan Pulks* was disbanded.

Blue Ulan Pulk (Graf Rudnicki)
Created early in 1745 with eight *Hof-Fahnen* [banners].

Commanders
1745 *Rudnicki*
1762 *Bielack*
1763 Disbanded

---

[111] Duffy (2008) 103 and
[112] Duffy (2008) 230
[113] Duffy (2008) 265-271

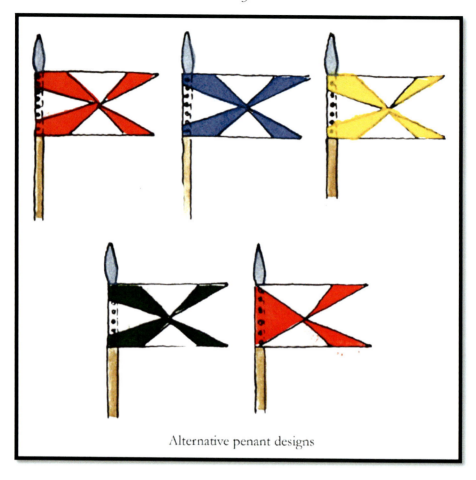

Alternative penant designs

Red Ulan Pulk (Graf Renard)
Raised 1743.

Commanders
1742 Wilzewsky/Wilozewsky
1757 *Renard*
1759 *Schiebel*
1763 disbanded

Yellow Ulan Pulk (Graf Bertuszewsky)
Raised in 1745. During the Seven Years War, this Pulk remained in Poland.

Commanders
1745 *Bertuszewski*
1750 *Bronikowski*
1768 Disbanded

Ulan Uniform 1741-63

In 1741 the Ulan uniform was first regulated.

HEADWEAR: White cone formed cap, the top flat, and a band of fur around the bottom.

COAT: White calf-length caftan coat with low upstanding collar in facing colour. By the 1750s, the *Ulan* wore a more uniform style tailcoat with lapels and turnbacks in the facing colour.

BUTTONS: Four brass buttons on the lapels, two on the cuff-flap.

CUFFS: White with wide cuff-flaps in facing colour.

TURNBACKS: Facing colour.

LEGWEAR: Long wide trousers like the Cossack *Sharavas* reaching to the ankles in the facing colour. Black boots.

EQUIPMENT: Natural leather cross-belt, waist-belt and cartridge box,

SIDEARMS: Each *Pocztowi* (servants) was issued a pistol and cartridge box and every *Towarczy* (Polish noble) in addition received a carbine. Each individual provided their own sabre and lance. The sabre had a black scabbard with brass fittings. The lance pennant was white and facing colour.

HORSE FURNITURE: Fur cloth. The un-dyed blanket roll was in front of the saddle: on the back a big fodder sack hanging down on both sides.

Kettledrummers
Each *Pulk* had a kettle-drummers equipped with brass kettle-drums.

Trumpeters
Each *Hof-Fahne* had at least one trumpeter.

Trumpeter of the Yellow Ulan Pulk Blendowski 1742

Table 22: Saxon Ulan Pulks

Ulan	Coat	Cuffs & Lapels	Waistcoat & trousers	buttons
Red Ulan Pulk *Wilzewsky/Wilozewsky* (1742-57) *Renard* (1757-59), *Schiebel* (1759-63) Disbanded 1763	white	red	red	white metal
Blue Ulan Pulk *Rutonitzki/Rudnicki* (1745-62) Disbanded 1763	white	blue	blue	white metal
Yellow Ulan Pulk *Blendowski/Blendowsky* (1742-50) *Bronikowski* (1751-63) Disbanded 1768	white	yellow	yellow	white metal
Disbanded in 1748				
Black Ulan Pulk *Sychodzinsky/Sichodrinski* (1740-45) *Borzislawsky/Boroslavski* (1745-48) Disbanded 1748	white	black	white	white metal
Green Ulan Pulk *Bertuszewsky/Bertuszewski* (1745-48) Disbanded 1748	white	green	green	white metal
White Ulan Pulk *Uhlan* (1745-48) Disbanded 1748	white	white	white	white metal

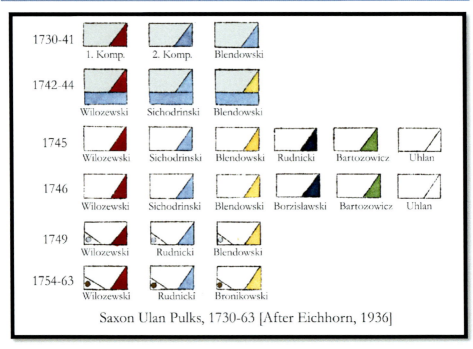

Saxon Ulan Pulks, 1730-63 [After Eichhorn, 1936]

Saxon Army 1740-1763

Officer of the Red Ulan Pulk, 1763

Ulan Officer Uniform

HEADWEAR: Black fur cap.

COAT: White tunic with wide long sleeves.

FACINGS: Upstanding collar with laces, and lining in facing colour.

TURNBACKS: Long blue turnbacks with a crowned "*AR*" in the same blue-white lace.

LACE: Facing colour and white

BUTTONS: Six silver buttons in 1-2-3 pattern on the breast.

WAISTCOAT: Blue waistcoat with blue-white lacing along edges.

SASH: White-red sash.

LEGWEAR: Blue baggy trousers reaching to the ankles. Black boots without spurs.

SIDEARMS: Curved sabre with black scabbard, brass handle and fittings. All bearded, but no pigtails.

HORSE FURNITURE: Pointed saddlecloth in facing colour with wide silver border

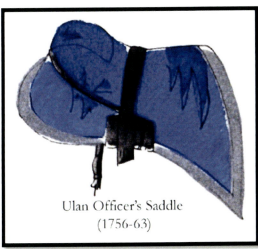

Ulan Officer's Saddle (1756-63)

Chapter 12:
New Saxon Cavalry Regiments (1761-63)

Reiter Regiment

A regiment of cavalry was established on 31 March 1761 after the renewal of the Franco-Saxon Convention with paper strength of 659 men in four squadrons (eight companies). The personnel were drawn from the dismounted *Garde du Corps* and cuirassiers serving as grenadier companies of the infantry.[114] The regiment was either referred to as the *Reiter* Regiment or the Schleiben (Cuirassier) Regiment after its commander.[115]

The (new) *Reiter Regiment* 1761-63 had eight companies. This gave a strength of 659 all ranks.[116]

> **Regimental staff** (19 men):
> 1 *Oberst*, 1 *Oberst-Lt*, 2 Major, 1 *Regiments-Quartiermeister*, 2 *Aides-Majors*, 1 *Auditeur*, 1 *Chirurgen Major* [surgeon], 1 *Almosenier*, 1 kettledrummer, 1 provost, 1 *Wagenmeister*, 1 *Sattler*, 5 servants.
>
> **8 Companies** (8 companies of 80 = 640 men):
> 6 captains, 2 staff-captains, 8 lieutenants, 8 *Kornet*, 16 *Wachtmeister*, 8 *Standart-Junker*, 8 *Feldscher*, 8 *Fourier*, 8 *Marechaux*, 32 corporals, 16 trumpeters and 520 troopers.

In 1764, the first two companies were reformed as Garde du Corps and the remaining six companies were used as cadres to re-raised the six cuirassier regiments and served as their Carabinier company.

Inhaber and Commander
1761 *GM Kaspar von Schlieben.*[117]
1762 Absent.

---

[114] Salisch (2009)
[115] Prince Xaver himself referred to the unit as "the new cavalry regiment," noting that its upkeep is costing him an arm and a leg. [Salisch (2009)]
[116] Hasse and Eichhorn (1936) 4
[117] He had been the commander of the *Rutowski Chevauleger Regiment*. On 23 July 1762, he was killed at Lutterberg

Saxon Army 1740-1763

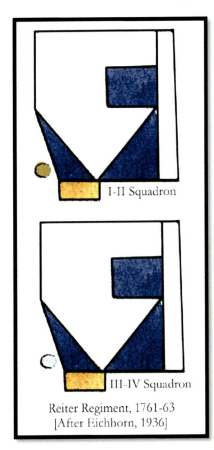

I-II Squadron
III-IV Squadron
Reiter Regiment, 1761-63
[After Eichhorn, 1936]

I-II Squadron Uniform[118]
HEADWEAR: Tricorn.
COAT: White coat with blue cuffs and turnbacks.
KOLLET: The Straw-coloured *Kollet* had blue lace with yellow central line.
WAISTCOAT: Blue waistcoat.
BUTTONS: Brass.
DISTINCTIONS: Musicians had reversed colours. Blue with straw facings and yellow lace.

III-V Squadrons Uniform
HEADWEAR: Tricorn.
COAT: White coat with blue cuffs and turnbacks.
KOLLET: The Straw-coloured *Kollet* had blue lace with white central line.
WAISTCOAT: Blue waistcoat.
BUTTONS: White metal.
LEGWEAR: Buff
DISTINCTIONS: Musicians had reversed colours. Blue with straw facings and white lace.

Campaign History
Their duty for the summer of 1761 was to protect foragers and the important work of securing the financial contributions from the Eisenach area. As the supply situation for the Saxon Corps deteriorated, the desertion among the infantry became a problem. This situation caused quite a number of the infantrymen to attempt desert, so the cavalry were involved in apprehending fugitives.

In 1762, the regiment around Kassel. On 14 July it assisted in repulsing a Prussian thrust at Luckner near Melsungen. On the 23 July, it was heavily engaged in the second battle of Lutterberg, where Oberst von Schlieben was killed. In January 1763 the regiment stood at over 600 men. In late March, the regiment of 880 troopers (640 mounted) were split into six detachments for their return to Saxony.

---

[118] Schirmer (1989) III: 15 and Eichhorn (1936)

Frei-Husaren von Schill Squadron

Raised in 1761 by the former Austrian cavalry officer, Rittmeister von Schill who was the father of Major von Schill who led an uprising against Napoleon in 1809. On campaign, it served as Prince Xaver's *Leib-Garde* squadron. This unit also included a number of mounted and foot *Jäger*.

Uniform[119]

HEADWEAR: Red mirliton had a black edged white bag and white over red plume.

DOLMAN: Yellow dolman with white lace.

PELISSE: White pelisse with red lace and brown fur.

LEGWEAR: Red breeches with white Hungarian knots and lace, black hussar boots edged white.

SABRETACHE: Red sabretache with white "*AR*" cipher and crown surrounded by yellow and white lace.

EQUIPMENT: Brown leather waist-belt.

SIDE-ARMS: Sabre with steel fittings and brown leather scabbard.

Husar vom Freikorps des Obersten von Schill, 1761

---

[119] Trache (c1900), Schirmer (1989: III-15) and Friedrich (1998: 98) agree that this was the Seven Years War Uniform despite Knötel showing them in green dolman and pelisse. This was their uniform after the Seven Years War.

Chapter 13
Cavalry Standards

The precise appearance of flags and standards are difficult to determine without surviving examples. The representations in the literature often contradict.

During the Second Silesian War, the following standards were lost by the Saxon Cavalry.
- Two standards of KR Bestenbostel and one standard of KR von Gersdorff at Hohenfriedberg (4 June 1745).
- One standard of KR O'Byrn and one standard from either KR Dallwitz or Vitzthum were captured at Hennersdorf (23 Nov 1745).
- One standard at Kesselsdorf (15 Dec 1745).

In 1753, the cuirassier regiment received new standards. The *Garde du Corps* and the *Chevauleger* retained their standards.

Under the terms of the Pirna capitulation Saxony's regimental flags and standards were laid up in the neutral Königstein Fortress for the duration of the war. However it seems that the re-formed units of Xaver's corps were issued new flags in Vienna before marching off to join the French. These were simpler, painted versions of their old embroidered flags. Only the lost standard of "New" Reiter Regiment at Lutterberg (23 July 1762) was officially captured.

Each cavalry squadron had a rectangular standard carried by the cornet. Friedrich (1998) shows two cavalry standard-bearers with the wide "baldrics" in the same metallic colour as the buttons (i.e. silver or gold) and a central stripe of the regimental facing colour.[120] Earlier Saxon infantry colour bearers in the 1730s are shown in with what appear to be narrow plain buff leather baldrics.

---

[120] Friedrich (1998)

Guard Cavalry Standards
Garde du Corps Standard
The Garde du Corps carried four white damask *Leibstandarten* and did not have a *Regimentsstandarte*.

M1730 *Leibstandarte*
The white standards were embroidered with gold and had a gold fringe.
OBVERSE: The Electoral Saxon coat of arms and electoral coronet was surrounded by green palm leaves. The left side of the shield was black over white with two red crossed swords. In the right side were nine alternating yellow-black stripes with diagonal green band.
REVERSE: The Royal Polish arms and crown was surrounded by green palm leaves. The red shield was quartered: top left and on the bottom right was the Polish white eagle, on the top right and bottom left was the white knight.

M1752 *Leibstandarte*
OBVERSE: The Electoral Saxon arms as above.
REVERSE: The centre device had the golden "*AR*" royal cipher on a pedestal surmounted by a royal crown and surrounded by green palm leaves.

M1752 *Liebstandarte* of the Garde du Corps

Karabinier-Garde Regiment Standard
The regiment carried a *Leibstandarte* and three *Regimentsstandarte*.
Leibstandarte: White standard with gold AR, crown and fringes.
Regimentsstandarte: Ponceau red standard with gold AR, crown and fringes.

Cuirassier Standards
M1730 Cuirassier Standards
OBVERSE: Electoral Saxon coat of arms surrounded by green palm leaves.
REVERSE: Royal Polish coat of arms surrounded by green palm leaves.

M1730 pattern Cuirassier *Ordinärstandarte* of the CL1 Leib-Regiment, 1740-48

Table 23: M1730 standards.[121]
Saxon coat of arms on one side and the Polish coat of arms.

	Field	Obverse	Reverse	Decorations
KR1 *Kronprinz*	dark blue [*blau*]	Saxon coat of arms	Polish coat of arms	gold
KR2 *Prinz Friedrich*	*paille* [light buff]	Saxon coat of arms	Polish coat of arms	gold
KR3 *Polenz*	canel / brown [*braun*]	Saxon coat of arms	Polish coat of arms	gold
"**KR-iv**" *Kriegen*	"Jonquil" yellow	Saxon coat of arms	Polish coat of arms	gold
New standards issued to four regiments in 1732				
"**KR-v**" *Promnitz*	sky blue [*bleumourant*]	Saxon coat of arms	Polish coat of arms	gold
"**KR-vi**" *Nassau*	sky blue [*bleumourant*]	Saxon coat of arms	Polish coat of arms	gold
"**KR-vii**" *Brand*	white	"AR" cipher	"AR" cipher	gold
"**KR-viii**" *Sachsen-Gotha*	white	Saxon coat of arms	"AR" cipher	gold

---

[121] Hasse & Eichhorn (1936) 7

In 1730, the four-cuirassier regiments were issued with seven standards carried by each of the companies including the *Karabinier* Company that carried the white *Leibstandarte*. In 1732, the *Karabinier* Company was disbanded so their *Leibstandarte* was carried by the first company. In 1732, the four new Cuirassier Regiments raised in 1732 were issued with standards and had minor variations as indicated in Table 23.

In 1740, the number of standards was reduced to three standards per regiment with one standard allocated per squadron. The *Leibstandarte* was now carried by the first squadron. Uniformity could not be maintained by the frequent changes.[122]

Table 24: Saxon Cuirassier Standards in 1745.[123]

	Leibstandarte	*Ordinärstandarte*	Decorations
KR1 *Leib-Regiment*	light blue [*hellblau*]	light blue	gold
KR2 *Prinz Friedrich*	yellow	white	gold
KR3 *von Vitzthum*	not known	not known	
"**KR-iv**" *Haudring*	yellow	yellow	silver
"**KR-v**" *von O'Byrn*	not known	not known	
"**KR-vi**" *Minkwitz*	yellow	yellow	silver
"**KR-vii**" *L'Annonciade*	green	white	silver
"**KR-viii**" *Senssdorff*	not known	not known	

In 1748, there was an exchange of standards with those in main armoury in Dresden took place. Each regiment had a white *Leibstandarte* and three *Regimentsstandarten* that matched their new facings colours.

Table 25: M1748 Cuirassier Standard.[124]

	Leibstandarte	*Regimentsstandarte*	Decorations and fringe
KR1 *Leib-Cuirassier Regt.*	white	red [*rot*]	gold
KR2 *Königlich Prinz*	white	sky blue [*bleumourant*]	silver
KR3 *von Vitzthum*	white	dark blue [*dunkelblau*]	gold
KR4 *von Arnim*	white	orange	silver
KR5 *von Plötz*	white	green [*grün*]	silver
KR6 *von Rechenberg*	white	yellow [*gelb*]	silver

---

[122] Hasse & Eichhorn (1936) 7
[123] Hasse & Eichhorn (1936) 7.
[124] Hasse & Eichhorn (1936) 7

Saxon Army 1740-1763

Standard-bearer of the
KR4 Rechenberg, 1748

1752 Standards

In 1752, the cuirassier regiments received new standards at the Camp of Ubigau in the facing colour and embroidery in button colour. Each regiment had a white *Leibstandarte* with the Saxon-Polish coat of arms and three *Ordinärstandarten* in facing colour with the royal cipher and crown. All standards were embroidered in gold regardless of button colour. The cords, tassels and fringes were mixed with crimson silk instead of plain gold or silver in the earlier standards. The staves were painted vermillion red. The standard belts were covered with velvet in the facing colour and decorated in gold or silver tresses in accordance to the button colour. These belts were normally covered in waterproof oilcloth lined with green linen cloth for campaign.

Liebfahne: White field. The centre device was an ornate gold shield upon a wreath of green palm leaves, on top a gold crown lined crimson, set with silver pearls and coloured stones. The shield had a red field with the arms of Poland [the eagle and the knight in white] and in the centre was the Saxon coat of arms beneath the electoral hat.

Ordinarfahne: Field was in facing colour. The centre the "AR" cipher was in button colour surmounted by a crimson lined gold crown set with silver pearl and coloured stones on a white pedestal surrounded by green palm leaves, a gold design around the border. The fringe was crimson and button colour.

KR1 Leib-Regiment   KR3 Vitzthum
M1752 Cuirassier Regimentsstandarte

After the capitulate ion at Lilienstein, the standards were laid up in Fortress Königstein where they were remained until 1763 when they were handed over then to the newly formed Kürassier-regiments.

Table 26: M1752 Cuirassier Standards.

Regiment	Field	"AR" Cipher	Fringe
KR1 *Leib-regiment*	poppy red	gold	gold-crimson
KR2 *Kurprinz*	sky blue [*bleumourant*]	silver	silver-crimson
KR3 *von Vitzthum*	blue	gold	gold-crimson
KR4 *von Arnim*	crimson	gold	gold-crimson
KR5 *von Plötz*	green	gold	gold-crimson.
KR6 *Fürst Anhalt*	yellow	silver	silver-crimson

Dragoon Standards

In 1730, each dragoon regiment had six flags of the same design distinguished by their field colour. The Grenadier Company carried the white *Leibfahne*. In 1733, supposedly DR2 von Katte received *paille* flags when they changed to yellow facings. Whether all flags were substituted is doubtful.[125]

Dragoon flag, c1710

Dragoon flag, c1730

Table 27: Dragoon flags in 1730.[126]

	Field	Embroidery
DR1 *von Arnstädt*	dark blue [*dunkelblau*]	Silver
DR2 *von Katte*	parrot green [*papageigrün*]	silver
DR3 *Goldacker*	grass green [*grasgrün*]	silver
DR4 *Chevalier de Saxe*	sky blue [*bleumourant*]	silver

---

[125] Hasse and Eichorn (1936) 10
[126] Hasse and Eichhorn (1936) 10

DR4 Chevalier de Saxe standard (1730-45)

DR3 von Schlichting standard (1734-45)

In 1743, a flag of the DR4 Chevalier de Saxe was described as *bleumourant* [sky blue] with silver "AR" cipher, crown and palm leaves surrounded with crimson and silver fringe. This seems to suggest that they received new flags.[127]

In 1745 the DR3 Schlichting Dragoons received one white *Leibstandarte* and a blue standard to replace the *Leibstandarte* and the red standard that had been lost at Hohenfriedberg on 4 June 1745.[128]

In 1746 the DR1 Rechenberg received two yellow flags instead of the exhausted blue ones. In 1747 DR2 Sondershausen handed in their yellow flags for one white Leibfahne with coat of arms and three new green flags with "*AR3*" monogram.[129]

Table 28: 1745 Dragoon flags in 1746.[130]

	Field	Embroidery
DR1 *Rechenberg*	yellow [*gelb*]	silver
DR2 *Sondershausen*	green [*grün*]	silver
DR3 von *Schlichting* / *Von Arnim* (1745)	blue [*blau*]	silver
DR4 *von Plötz*	red [*rot*]	silver

---

[127] Hasse and Eichhorn (1936) 10
[128] Hasse & Eichhorn (1936) 10
[129] Hasse & Eichhorn (1936) 10
[130] Hasse & Eichhorn (1936) 10

"New" Reuter Regiment

In 1761 the newly formed cavalry regiment received two light blue [*hellblau*] standards that were probably made in France. It is unknown whether they were painted or embroidered. One of these was lost at Lutterberg (23 July 1762).[131]

Chevauleger Flags

The Chevauleger carried one *Liebfahne* and three *Ordinarfahne*. The Chevauleger were not issued new flags in 1753.[132]

Fahne of CL1 Prinz Carl Chevauleger, c1735

Liebfahne: White field with centre device of an ornate gold shield upon a wreath of green palm leaves. On top of the shield was a gold crown, lined crimson, set with silver pearls and coloured stones. On the shield was a red field on which the arms of Poland (eagle and knight) are in white, on the centre the arms of Saxony beneath the electoral hat.

Ordinarfahne – Field in facing colour with the centre the monogram of "AR" in button colour, crimson lined gold crown set with silver pearl and coloured stones on a pedestal in white surrounded by pale green palm leaves, a gold design around the border, fringe in crimson and button colour.

Table 29: Chevauleger *Ordinärfahne*.

Regiment	Issued	Ordinärfahne	Cipher	Fringe	Fineals
CL1 *Prinz Carl*	6 May 1735	Red [*rot*]	AR3	gold & crimson	gold
CL2 *Graf Brühl*	1748	sky blue [*bleumourant*]	AR3	Gold	gold
CL3 *Albrecht*	1747	crimson [*ponceaurot*]	AR3	Gold	gold
CL4 *Rutowski*	May 1743	Red [*rot*]	AR3	gold & black	gold

---

[131] Hasse and Eichorn (1936) 10
[132] Pengel & Hurt (1981)

Saxon Army 1740-1763

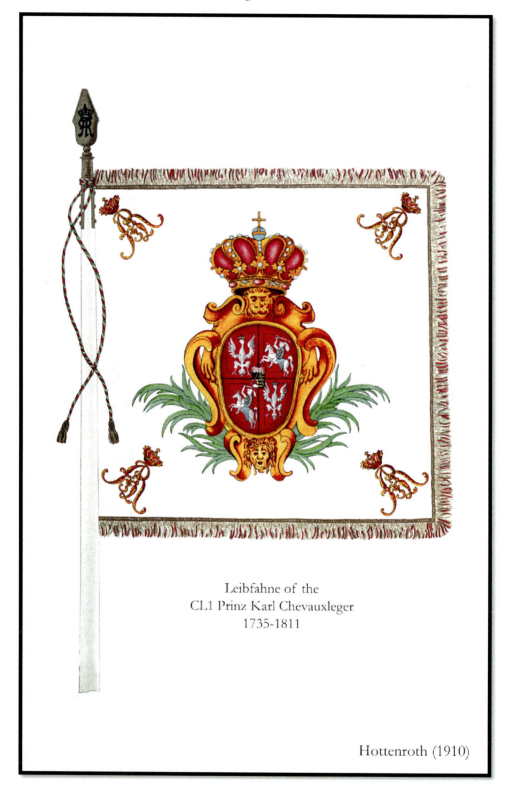

Leibfahne of the
CL1 Prinz Karl Chevauxleger
1735-1811

Hottenroth (1910)

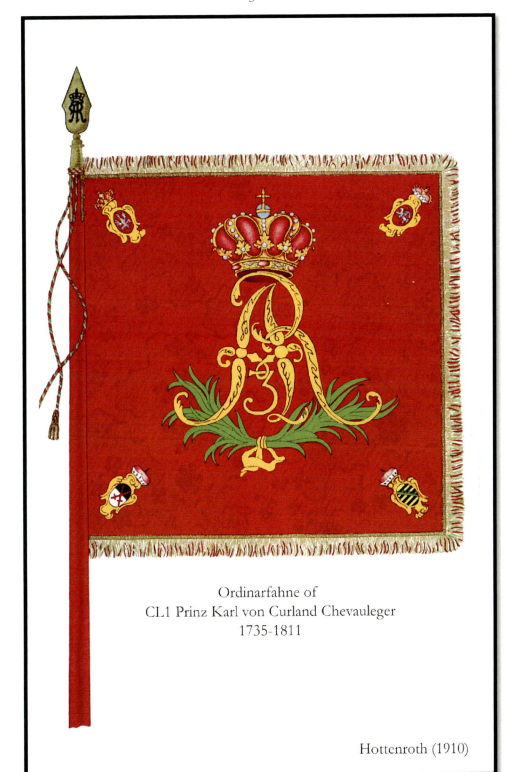

Ordinarfahne of
CL1 Prinz Karl von Curland Chevauleger
1735-1811

Hottenroth (1910)

Saxon Army 1740-1763

CL2 Graf Brühl
Leibhahne

CL2 Graf Brühl
Ordinarfahne

CL3 Albrecht
Leibhahne

CL3 Albrecht
Ordinarfahne

After Hottenroth (1910)

Saxon Army 1740-1763

Standartjunker der Prinz-Albrecht-Chevauxlegers 1745-1753

Ulan Standards

Standards had a white cross on the field in facing colour on the pole with a gilded button.

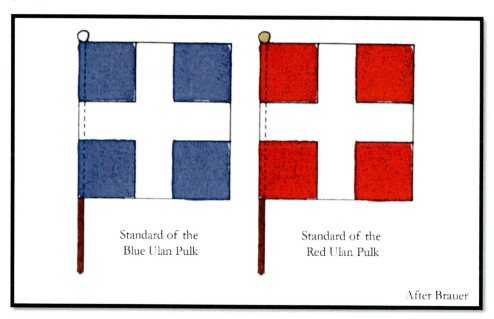

Chapter 14: Artillery

The Saxon artillery underwent frequent changes during the period. From 1730 the artillery was divided in an artillery battalion with three gunner companies as well as the fourth company, consisting of *Mineuren* [miners], *Pontonieren* and craftsmen. The Gunner Company (56 men) had 1 *Kapitän*, 1 *Premier-Leutnant*, 1 *Sous-Leutnant*, 1 *Stück-Junker*, 1 *Kanonier-Sergeant*, 3 *Kanonier-Korporale*, 1 *Feuerwerks-Korporal*, 9 *Feuerwerker*, 2 *Kanonier-Tamboure* (drummers), 36 *Kanoniere* (gunners).

Leibfahne   Ordinarfahne

Flags of the Artillery Corps 1752-1810 [Hottenroth, 1910]

Every gunner company had a *Füsilier* company of 85 men attached who were responsible for the close defence of the ordnance and acted as auxiliaries to the trained gunners. It was usual that half the gun crew consisted of fusiliers and at times infantrymen were also used.

In 1756, the artillery comprised the:
Haus-Kompagnie [Dresden Arsenal and Fortress personnel]
Artillery Battalion of 4 companies (about 600 men)
Ingenieurkorps [Engineers],
Mineurs (9 men), *Pontonier* (28 men), *Handwerker* (workers)
Rosspartie [artillery train] (223 men and 627 horses).

The guns used during the War of Polish Succession and the War of Austrian Succession consisted of 3-, 6-and 12-pdr cannon and of 8-, 16-, and 24-pdr howitzers. The gun batteries were at 500-1000 paces. These were mainly the M1733 pattern guns but older guns were still in service.

Saxon Army 1740-1763

In 1756, the Saxon artillery park had 12 x M1730 24-pdrs siege guns [10-horse team] 27 x Heavy M1730 12-pdrs [10 or 12-horse team], 4 x Heavy M1730 6-pdrs and 4 x 24-pdr howitzers with a 10-horse team.[133]

Gun Carriages

The Saxon gun carriages were stained black with a mixture of asphalt [by-product from burnt mineral oils], litharge [lead (II) oxide], boiled linseed oil ad turpentine. This gave the appearance of a very dark almost black weathered creosote appearance. The metal fittings were yellow metal (i.e. brass) or painted dark yellow.[134] The bridle of the teams was not regulated and most came with the hired draught animals.

Artillery Uniform (1740-63)

In 1717, the Saxon Artillery adopted the medium-green coat with poppy red distinctions that was characteristic of their dress until 1914. This contrasted with the dark green used by the Russians.[135]

Officer of the Artillery Corps, 1748-56

HEADWEAR: Black tricorn with yellow trim. Bombardiers wore a bombardier's hat.

STOCK: Black stock

COAT: Medium-green coats with poppy red facings and brass buttons. Buff waistcoats. White linen shirt.

WAISTCOAT: From 1732 gunners, the *Feuerwerker* and Pontonier had green waistcoats. Fusilier had red waistcoats.

BREECHES: Buff breeches and black gaiters. White breeches were worn in summer.

DISTINCTIONS: Officers wore gold trim to the tricorn and gold braid.

EQUIPMENT: Buff belts.

SIDEARMS: Straight bladed short sword. Bombardiers also had a pistol. Muskets were carried for guard duty.

Artillerie-Fuhrwesen [Artillery Driver]:

HEADWEAR: Plain black tricorn.

COAT: White coat without lapels with green facings and brass buttons.

---

[133] Summerfield (2009) 41 & 43
[134] Summerfield (2009) 24
[135] See Summerfield (2009) *Saxon Artillery 1733-1827*, Partizan Press.

Saxon Army 1740-1763

WAISTCOAT: Green waistcoat,
LEGWEAR: Straw-coloured trousers and long boots.

Armee-Fuhrwesen [Army driver]:
HEADWEAR: Plain black tricorn.
COAT: White coat without lapels with red facings and brass buttons.
WAISTCOAT: Red waistcoat,
LEGWEAR: Straw-coloured trousers and long boots.

Pontonnier (1745) and Miner (1748).

Chapter 15:
Saxon Quick-Fire Guns

The Saxons with their *Geschwindstück* that literally means "quick-fire piece" had the most advanced elevating system in Europe at that time. [136] It allowed the gun to double its rate of fire of canister over a gun using elevating wedges. It was also referred to as the *Schnellschiesser* or *Geschwindgeschütz* in other countries such as Austria and Prussia. These types of cannon belong to the class of so entitled *Einfallendes Geschütz* [literally 'dropping cannon'] and was probably a Saxon invention.

Geschwindstück

In the 1720s, **GL Franz Karl Obmaus**[137] designed the *Obmaus Geschwindschuss-Maschine* [quick fire elevating system].[138] In July 1728, Augustus II of Saxony presented Frederick William I of Prussian with two 2-pdr *Einfallende Geschütze* during his stay in Dresden.[139]

3-pdr Geschwindstück

In 1734, the M1734 *Geschwindstück* of 22 calibres (76mm, 158cm long and 240kg) was introduced into service.[140] The *Protzkasten* [Limber Box] contained fixed ammunition on the limber. It could be loaded in two different ways.

> **FIRING CANISTER:** The gunner would remove the wedge to allow the breech to drop to about 45 degrees to rest upon the axle of the gun carriage and the canister round was placed into the cannon without the need to employ the rammer. The breech was lifted back and locked into its previous firing position before being fired.
>
> **FIRING SHOT**: the gun was loaded in the conventional manner with the rammer.

The 3-pdr *Geschwindstücke* fitted with the Obmaus *Richtmaschine* saw service with the Saxon Auxiliary Corps in the 1737 campaign along the Danube. At Radojovac (28 Sept. 1737) in Serbia, the Saxon 3-pdr *Geschindstücke* in particular decided the action because their sustained rapid canister-fire had such devastate effect against the densely packed Turkish Spahis according to the report FM Khevenhüller.[141]

In 1741, the Saxons mobilised twenty M1730 3-pdrs at a ratio of one piece per infantry battalion rather than two.

---

[136] See Rogge and Summerfield (2012) for a more detailed discussion of these artillery pieces.
[137] **GL Franz Karl Obmaus** was the *Chef* of the Saxon Artillery until his death in 1735.
[138] Decker (1822) *Geschichte des Geschützwesens und der Artillerie in Europa*, Berlin, p59
[139] Dr. Moritz Meyer (1835), *Handbuch zur Geschichte der Feuerwaffen-Technik*, Berlin
[140] Anon (1840) *Archiv für die Officiere der Königlich Preußischen Artillerie und dem Ingenieur-Korps*, Vol. 11, Berlin.
[141] Streufflers (1828) *Oesterreichische Militätische Zeitschrift*, vol. III, Vienna, p347

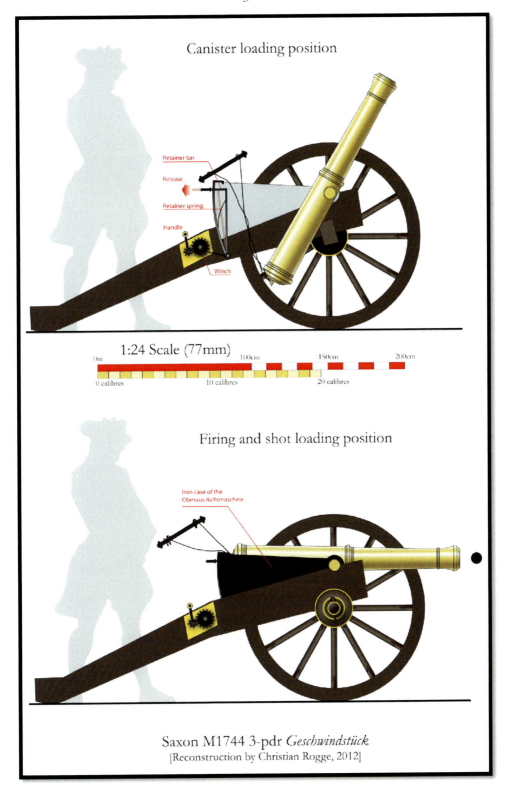

Saxon M1744 3-pdr *Geschwindstück*
[Reconstruction by Christian Rogge, 2012]

At Hohenfriedberg (4 June 1745), the Saxons had 44x 3-pdr *Geschwindstücke* allocated at two pieces per infantry Bn.¹⁴² The Grenadier Bns had no artillery pieces. The Saxons lost 27x 3-pdr *Geschwindstücke* in the battle. These were put into store in a Silesian Fortress and used a decade later during the Seven Years War by the Prussians.

Saxon M1744 3-pdr *Geschindstück* [1:24 Scale]
[Reconstruction by Christian Rogge, 2012]

In 1744, the M1744 3-pdr *Geschwindstück* was reduced to 20 calibres (145cm) long to allow the loading of canister easier.

6-pdr Geschwindstück

To replace the lost 3-pdrs, the M1745 6-pdr of 16 calibres (145cm long) was produced. Each infantry Bn had two M1745 6-pdr *Geschwindstück* battalion guns served by eight gunners and had a 4-horse team. Some of the second battalions were equipped with M1744 3-pdr *Geschwindstück* instead. On 15 December 1745, the deadly canister fire from the Saxon *Geschwindstücke* at the battle of Kesselsdorf almost caused the collapse of the Prussian attack on the Saxon centre. The Saxons lost 46 pieces including 10x M1745 6-pdr, 21x M1744 3-pdr and 1x 2-pdr *Geschwindstücke*.¹⁴³

In 1756, there were 50 M1746 6-pdr *Geschwindstücke* with the army of 1756. Each of the 25 regular field-battalions had two pieces. The combined grenadier battalions were not allocated guns.

Geschwindstücke in Prussian Service

In 1746, Prussia built two M1746 *Oettner* 3-pdrs based on the Saxon *Geschwindstück*. Frederick II rejected this design of regimental artillery. During the Seven Years War, the Prussians used over eighty former Saxon pieces including the M1734 and M1744 3-pdr *Geschwindstück* gun tubes that had been stored in a Silesian Fortress. These received a cascable and were mounted on conventional Prussian carriages that used elevating wedges rather than the Obmaus *Richtmaschine*. In 1757, the newly raised Prussian Infantry Regiments from men from of the former Saxon army received 46x Saxon 6-pdr *Geschwindstücke* captured at Pirna and four other 3-pdrs to give a total of 50 regimental guns.¹⁴⁴

---

¹⁴² Streufflers (1828) *Oesterreichische Militätische Zeitschrift*, vol. III, Vienna.
¹⁴³ entitled *Einfallende Kanonen,*
¹⁴⁴ Schöning, Kurd Wolfgang von, (1844) *Historisch-biographische Nachrichten zur Geschichte der Brandenburg-Preußischen Artillerie*, Volume II, Berlin, p33 [Translated by Christian Rogge]

Sardinian 4-pdr "Cannone alla Sassone"

In 1751, Captain Casimiro Gabaleone di Salmour designed the M1751 4-pdr "*Cannone alla Sassone*"[145] [77mm and 144cm long] based on the Saxon *Geschwindstück* for the Kingdom of Sardinia. By 1759, a total of 89 regimental guns had been cast.[146] Interestingly, Austria, France, Sardinia-Piedmont and Suvorov's Russians used them as mountain guns during the Italian Campaigns (1792-1800). Later the Italian Republic (1802-05) and Kingdom of Italy (1805-10) employed them.[147]

French 4pdr "*à la Suédoise*" (1757-63)

By October 1757, Prince Xavier formed a new Saxon Army of 7,331 men in Hungary. The grenadiers of IR9 Fürst Lubomirski and IR2 Prinz Sachsen-Gotha were reformed from former gunners. In August 1758 these grenadier companies were used to form two new artillery companies of 125 men. Maria Josepha of Saxony (1731–67)[148] donated sixteen French M1757 4-pdr "*à la Suédoise*" battalion guns bearing her coat of arms. Each of the fifteen infantry battalions had one 4pdr "*à la Suédoise*" with one piece in reserve.

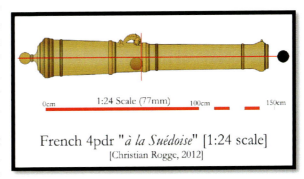

French 4pdr "*à la Suédoise*" [1:24 scale]
[Christian Rogge, 2012]

By September 1758, the new Saxon Auxiliary Corps in French pay joined De Contades Army in Westphalia. In the summer of 1761, the artillery was augmented to thirty guns giving two pieces each for the reorganised twelve line and three grenadier battalions. In 1763, the Saxon Army finally returned home and the 4pdr "*à la Suédoise*" guns were returned to the Strasbourg Arsenal having performed with honour.[149]

New M1766 Quick-Fire Guns

An updated version of the Obmaus *Richtmaschine* was used on the M1766 4-pdr *Schnellfeuergeschütze* [quick fire gun] and the M1766 4-pdr *Granatstück* that were still in use with the Saxon Army until 1812. According to Rouvroy (1809), this innovative system permitted a maximum of six to nine canister rounds per minute for a short period before the barrels would dangerously overheat. This was at least doubled the rate of fire for conventional artillery pieces. Other ammunition was loaded and rammed in the conventional manner.[150]

---

[145] Literally "Cannon of Saxon type."
[146] **Casimiro Gabaleone di Salmour** became Master General of Ordnance for the Kingdom of Sardinia. His elder brother, **Giuseppe Antonio Gabaleone**, was minister to the Elector of Saxony. [Giovanni Cerino-Badone (2011) *Private Communication*]
[147] Summerfield (2011) *SOJ-3*, p55; Duffy (1999) *Eagles over the Alps*, Emperor's Press, p30.
[148] **Maria Josepha of Saxony (1731-67)** was the second wife of the Louis, Dauphin of France (1729–1765) who were the parents of Louis XVI, Louis XVIII and Charles X.
[149] Summerfield (2009) 45-46.
[150] Summerfield (2009) 99-108 and Rouvroy (1809).

Chapter 16: Engineer Corps

It was established in 1681 for the construction and maintenance of the fortresses. On 9 May 1705, Jean de Bodt[151] became Commander of Engineers. In 1712, it was officially named *Ingenieurkorps* [Engineer Corps]. In 1730, the Engineer Corps had 39 officers and 5 NCOs:

1 *Generalleutnant* (lieutenant-general), 3 *Oberste* (colonels), 3 *Oberst-Leutnante* (lieutenant-colonels), 4 *Majore* (majors), 13 *Kapitäne* (captains), 15 *Ingenieure* (*Premier* and *Sous-Leutnante*), 5 *Kondukteure* (NCOs).

In 1742, the *Ingenieur-Akademie* [Engineer Academy] was created and was only merged with the *Artillerie-Akademie* in 1816. In 1743, the Corps was divided in two brigades, designed as:

Haus-Brigade (depot brigade) assigned to the maintenance and construction of military and civil buildings and fortification such as Torgau;
Feld-Brigade (Field-brigade) assigned to field service to create field defences, undertake sieges and produce maps.

At the end of the Second Silesian War in 1745, the corps was reduced in size.[152]

In October 1756, the Engineer Corps was disbanded upon the surrender at Pirna. The officers were sent home and NCOs entered Prussian service. A single *Festungs-Ingenieur* and a lieutenant remained in Saxon service at the Königstein fortress.

In 1763, at the end of the Seven Years' War, the Corps was re-raised with a Stab (command) of two brigades of 21 men:

Land-Brigade (*Festungs-Ingenieur*)
Feld-Brigade (*Pionier* and *Topographen*) plus five lecturers at the *Ingenieurs-Akademie*.

Uniforms of Engineer Officers

The engineers wore artillery uniform but with silver braid and buttons.[153]

HEADWEAR: Tricorn with silver hat lace and white cockade.

COAT: Steel green coats with silver lace on the cuffs and pockets. Brass gorget was introduced in 1748.

SASH: White, silver and red sash around the waste.

LEGWEAR: Black boots.

HORSE FURNITURE: Green with silver border.

---

[151] **Jean de Bodt** (1670-1745) born in Paris was a well-regarded military architect who had previously been in Prussian service. In 1706, he was promoted to *Oberst* [colonel.]
[152] Dr. Marco Pagan (11 Sept 2011) "Saxon Ingenieurkorps," *SYW Project*, www.kronoskaf.com/syw/ [Accessed 7 Oct 2011).
[153] Friedrich (1998) 20.

Saxon Army 1740-1763

Uniform of the NCOs.

COAT: Steel green coat. Poppy red collar, cuffs and turnbacks. No lapels.

BUTTONS: Silver (1:2:3)

DISTINCTIONS: Conductor had single silver lace and sergeants had double silver lace on the collar and cuffs.

WAISTCOAT: Red.

LEGWEAR: Red breeches, white gaiters and black shoes.

Engineer Corps, 1745-56 [After Trache]

Chapter 17:
Garrison and Invalid Companies

In September 1756, all eight Invalid Companies were concentrated at Königstein Fortress within the fortified Camp of Pirna.
    Königstein Fortress (one company of 195 men)
    Pleissenburg (one company of 115 men)
    Sonnenstein Fortress (one company of 125 men)
    Stolpen (one company)
    Waldheim (one company of 176 men)
    Wittenberg (three companies with a total of 354 men)

They were joined by the *Anhalt Frei-Company* of 116 formed from the men of the Wittenberg garrison. This garrison of Königstein did not participate in the attempted breakout on 16 October from the fortified Camp of Pirna. The neutral Fortress of Königstein was used to store the Saxon Army flags and standards. Only the Königstein and Sonnenstein Garrison Companies were not forcibly enlisted in the Prussian Army.

Invalid Company

HEADWEAR: Tricorn with white lace and red over blue pom-poms.
STOCK: Black stock.
COAT: Red coats with blue collar, cuffs, lapels and turnbacks.
WAISTCOAT: Blue waistcoat.
BUTTONS: White metal.
LEGWEAR: Blue trousers, black gaiters and black shoes.
EQUIPMENT: White leather belts and brass fittings.
DISTINCTIONS: NCOs had silver lace on the cuffs. Officers had sash, gorget and blue trousers.

Waldheim Invalid Company

HEADWEAR: Black tricorn.
STOCK: Red stock with white border.
COAT: Grey coats with red cuffs, lapels.
WAISTCOAT: Grey waistcoat.
BUTTONS: White metal.
LEGWEAR: Grey trousers, black gaiters and black shoes.
EQUIPMENT: White leather belts, brass fittings and *Pallasch* with black scabbard.
DISTINCTIONS: NCOs had silver lace on the cuffs.

Fortress Garrison Officers (1748-63).

HEADWEAR: Black tricorn with silver hat braid.
COAT: White coat with a row of ten buttons evenly spaced
COLLAR and CUFFS: Blue
WAISTCOATS: Blue waistcoats
BUTTONS: Silver buttons
LEGWEAR: Blue breeches, white gaiters and black shoes.

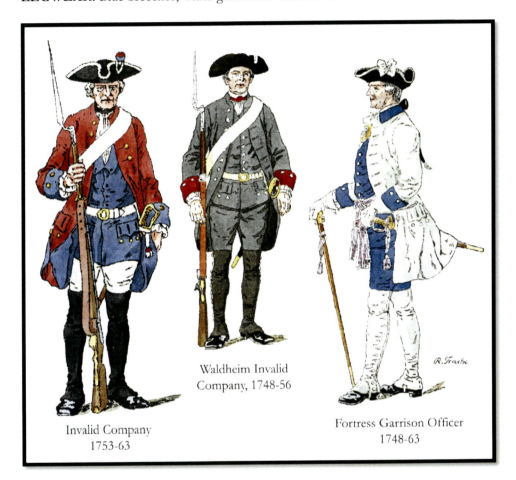

Invalid Company 1753-63
Waldheim Invalid Company, 1748-56
Fortress Garrison Officer 1748-63

Henneberg Militia

The County of Henneberg was separated from Saxony and consisted of a small strip of land in the heart of Franconia. For their own defence several companies of militia were raised in 1730 and disbanded in 1756.[154]

HEADWEAR: Black tricorn without hat lace.
STOCK: Black stock with white border.

---

[154] Lange quoted in Pengel & Hurt (1983) and Schirmer (1983) III-20.

Saxon Army 1740-1763

COAT: White coat with blue cuffs and turnbacks.
WAISTCOAT: Blue waistcoat.
BUTTONS: Brass buttons.
LEGWEAR: White breeches, grey stockings or black gaiters and black shoes.
EQUIPMENT: White belt with brass fittings, bayonet and sheath.
SIDEARMS: Troopers were armed with a musket, a bayonet and a sword.
DISTINCTIONS: NCOs had black tricorn with gold lace, blue coat with white collar and cuffs. The latter was edged with gold. They carried a halberd, a pistol on the left hip and a infantry sword on right hip.

Corporal and musketeer of the Henneberg Land Militia, 1748-56

Chapter 18:
Saxon Sidearms

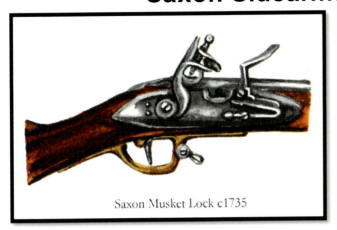

Saxon Musket Lock c1735

The stock of the musket was stained black or brown for fusiliers and polished walnut for grenadiers. The sling and lock covers were red leather.

Table 30: Saxon small-arms.[155]

	Calibre	Total Length	Barrel Length	Fittings	Origin
Infanterie-Gewehr					
M1705 Musket	18.4mm	145cm	103.5cm	Iron	Suhl
M1742 Musket	19-20mm	150cm	110cm	Brass	Suhl
M1763 Musket	18.5mm	144.5cm	106.3cm	Iron	Suhl
Grenadier Officer Carbine					
M1763	16.8mm	138cm	101.2cm	Brass	Suhl
Carbine					
M1705	18.8mm	132cm	93.7cm	Iron	Suhl
M1742	17.5mm	133.2cm	93cm	Brass	Olbemhan
M1745	19.3mm	139.5cm	99cm	Brass	Suhl, Heym
M1763	18.5mm	120cm	82cm	Brass	Suhl
Pistols					
M1705 Cavalry	18.5mm	53-55cm	34-35cm	Iron	Olbemhan
M1729 Cavalry	19.3mm	56cm	36.5cm	Brass	Olbemhan
M1742 NCO	17mm	46cm	26.5cm	Iron	Olbemhan
M1745 Dragoon	19-20mm	53-54cm	35-36cm	Brass	Heym
M1763 Cuirassier	19mm	45-46cm	27-28cm	Brass	Suhl, Heym

---

[155] Vollmer (2002) *Deutsche Militär-Handfeuerwaffen*, Volume II – Sachsen, Selbstverlag

Infantry Swords

All infantrymen at this time were issued with a sword (see p86) Infantry officers all carried a straight bladed sword as well as a partizan.

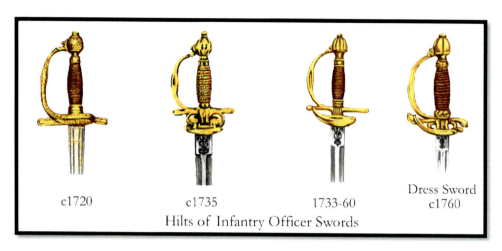

c1720   c1735   1733-60   Dress Sword c1760

Hilts of Infantry Officer Swords

Polearms

Corporal's Halberd   Sergeants' Half-Pike

18th Century Saxon NCO Polearms

Polearms were used to denote rank of Infantry Officers and NCOs.

NCOs who wore the same uniform as the ordinary soldier were equipped with a polearm. The *Kurz-Gewehr* [half pike] was used by company sergeants. The Halberd was carried by the corporal.

Officers carried partizans (or spontoons) with engraved heads and fringed depending upon rank. Grenadier officers had a special type of bayonet in the shape of a partizan. [See p31 for an illustration.

Bibliography

Adye R.W. and Eliot W.G. (1813 rp 2010) *Bombardier and Pocket Gunner*, T. Egerton, London [Reprint by Ken Trotman Publishing]

Anon (Sept-Oct 1959), "Plan der Koniglich Polnischen Kursachsichen Armee 1747," in *Zeitschirft fur Heereskunde*, No. 165

Anon (1788) "Plan, welcher das sächsische 4 pfündige Regts-Stück mit seiner Lafete enthält. (mit Erklärung)," *Neue Militärische Journal*, Book 1 Nr2, Plan II, Berlin [Translated by Christian Rogge (2009)]

Bleckwenn, H. (1987) *Die Friderischen Uniformen 1753-1786*, Volume IV – *Technische Truppen, Rückwärtiger Dienst, Kreigsformation*, Harenberg, Dortmund.

Brauer, Hans (1926-62) *Heer und Tradition*, Uniformbogen, No. 130-133 & 161-162 (Johannes Eichhorn), 163-165 (Johannes Eichhorn and Dr. Klietmann).

Cross, Otto (1902) *Prinz Xaver von Sachsen und das Korps bei der Franzosischen Amee 1758-1763*, University of Leipzig.

Czop, Jan (2009) *Barwa Wojska Rzeczypospolitej Obojga Narodow W XVIII Wieku*, Wydawnictwo Libra, Rzesziw, Poland.

Dawson A.L., Dawson P.L. and Summerfield S. (2007) *Napoleonic Artillery*, Crowood Press

Decker, Carl von (1822) *Gschichte des Geschutzens und der Artillerie in Europa von Ihrem*, Berlin

Dietrich, Walther (1927-33) *Die Uniformen der churfürstliche und königlich sächsischen Armee von 1682-1914*. M. Ruhl.

Friedrich W. (1998) *Die Uniformen der Kurfürstlich Sächsischen Armee 1683-1763*, Beyer Verlag, Dresden.

Guddat M. (1992) *Kanoniere, Bombardiere, Pontoniere: Die Artillerie Friedrich des Grossen*, Mittler & Sohn GmbH, Herford und Bonn.

Hasse, F. and Eichhorn, Johannes (1936) *Sächsieche Uniformen 1580-1914*, Dresden.

Hochedlinger, M. (2003) *Austria's War of Emergence, 1683-1797*, Pearson Education Ltd.

Hottenroth, Johann Edmund (1910) *Geschichte der Sächsischen Fahnen a und Standarten*, Dresden.

Jahns Max (1891) *Geschichte der Kriegswissen schaften vornehmlich in Deutschland*, Verl. von Oldenbourg, Munchen-Leipzig

Knötel R., Knötel H. and Sieg H. (1980) *Uniforms of the World 1700-1937*, Arms and Armour Press [Translation of (1937) *Handbuch der Uniformkunde*]

Kretschmar, A. von (1876 and 1879) *Geschichte der Kurfurstlich und Königlich Sachsischen Feld-Artillerie von 1620-1820*, Mittler, Berlin [(1876) Volume I (1620-1820): 146 pages and 2 plates and (1879) Volume II – 1821-1878 (360 and 9 plates)]

Lange (1981) "Saxon colours and cavalry standards," In P.D. Pengel (1981) *Seven Years War: Bavaria, Saxony and the Palatinate Supplement*, On Military Matters, USA

MacLagan, M. (1981) *Lines of Succession, Heraldry of the Royal Families of Europe*, MacDonald

Manley (1998) *War of Austrian Sucession, A Wargamer's Guide Part 9:* Uniforms of the *Denmark and German States*, OMM Publishing

Mollo J. (1977) *Uniforms of the Seven Years War 1756-63*, Blandford Press Ltd, Dorset

Müller R., Friedrich D. & W. (1984) *Die Armee Augusts des Starken: Das Sächische Heer von 1730-1733*, Berlin.

Müller R. and Rother W. (1991) *Die Kurfurstlich-Sächische Armee um 1791*, Berlin.

Nafziger G.F., Wesolowski MT and Devoe T (1991) *Poles and Saxons of the Napoleonic Wars*, Emperor's Press.

Pengel, R.D.
- (1979) *Uniforms of Swedish and German States: Cavalry of the Seven Years War*, On Military Matters, USA.
- (1979) *Uniforms of Swedish and German States: Infantry of the Seven Years War*, On Military Matters, USA.
- (1981) *Seven Years War: Bavaria, Saxony and the Palatinate Supplement*, On Military Matters, USA

Pivka O. von (1979) *Napoleon's German Allies (3): Saxony 1806-13*, Osprey

Rogge, C. and Summerfield S. (2012) "Saxon 18th Century Quick Fire Guns," *Smoothbore Ordnance Journal*, Issue 4.

Rouvroy, F. G. von (1809) *Vorlesungen über einen Theil der Geschützlehre, oder über den Bau und die Proporzionirung der Geschützröhre, Laffetten und Artilleriefuhrwerke, nebst deren Bespannung für die Königl. Sächs. Artillerieschule*, Dresden

Salisch, Marcus von (2009), *Treue Deserteure. Das kursächsische Militär und der Siebenjährige Krieg*, Munich

Schuster O. and Francke F. (1885) *Geschichte der Sachsischen Armee*, Leipzig.

Sturm Cigarette Cards
- (1932) *Deutsche Uniformen; Das Zeitalter Friedrich des Grossen*, Sturm Zigarettenfabrik, Dresden [Illustrations by Herbert Knötel and Text by Dr. Martin Lezius]
- (1932 rp2007) *The 'Sturm' Cigarette Cards of the German Uniforms of the Seven Years War*, Ken Trotman Publishing.

Summerfield, Stephen
- (2009) *Saxon Artillery 1733-1827*, Partizan Press.
- (2011) *Austrian Seven Years War Infantry and Engineers: Uniforms, Organisation and Equipment*, Ken Trotman Publishing.
- (2011) *Austrian Seven Years War Cavalry and Artillery: Uniforms, Organisation and Equipment*, Ken Trotman Publishing.

Tessin G. *Die Regimenter der Europaischen Staaten im Ancien regime des XVI. bis XVIII. Jahrhundrets.*

Vollmer, Udo (2002) *Deutsche Militär-Handfeuerwaffen*, Volume II – Sachsen, Selbstverlag,

Wilson P.H. (1998) *German Armies: War and German Politics 1648-1806*, UCL Press.

Wood J. (2007) *Armies and Uniforms of the Seven Years War, Volume 2: The Coalition Forces*, Partizan Press

Zamoyski, Adam (1987) *The Polish Way: A Thousand-Year History of the Poles and Their Culture*, John Murray.

Regimental Index

ARTILLERY		175--177

See Summerfield (2009) *Saxon Artillery 1733-1827*, Partizan Press for more details.

Artillery uniform	176
Gun Carriage Paint	176
Miner	177
Pontonier	177

CADETS	42

CAVALRY (NEWLY RAISED IN 1761)		158-160
Reiter Regiment	1761-63	158
Frei-Husaren von Schill Squadron	1761-63	160

CAVALRY STANDARDS	161-174
Chevauleger Flags	169
Cuirassier Standards	163
Dragoon Standards	167
Guard Cavalry Standard	162
Ulan Standards	174

CUIRASSIER REGTS (1740-63)			105-127
Arnim	KR6	1748-56	120
Bestenbostel	"KR-vii"	1745-46	116
Dallwitz	"KR-viii"	1733-41	117
Dessau-Anhalt	KR4	1749-56	118
Gersdorf	"KR-viii"	1741-45	117
Haudring	"KR-iv"	1740-46	114
Königlicher Prinz	KR2	1734-56	110
L'Annonciade	"KR-vii"	1746-48	116
Leib-Regiment	KR1	1733-56	107
Maffey	KR3	1738-45	112
Minckwitz	"KR-vi"	1745-48	116
Mitwitz	"KR-vii"	1735-45	116
Nassau	"KR-vi"	1731-45	116
O'Byrn	"KR-v"	1741-48	115
Plötz	KR5	1748-56	119
Promnitz	"KR-v"	1732-41	115
Rechenberg	KR4	1748	118
Ronnow	"KR-iv"	1746-48	114
Sachsen-Gotha	"KR-viii"	1733-41	117
Sondenhausen	KR4	1748-49	118
Vitzthum	KR3	1745-56	112

CUIRASSIER REGTS (RE-RAISED IN 1763)			
Arnim	KR6	1763-78	120
Benkendorf	KR3	1765-78	112
Brenkendorf	KR5	1764-78	119
Dessau-Anhalt	KR4	1763-86	118
Königlicher Prinz	KR2	1763	110
Kurfürst	KR1	1764-1806	107
Kurprinz	KR2	1763-64	110
Leib-Regt.	KR1	1763-64	107
Ronnow	KR2	1764-78	110
Vitzthum	KR3	1763-65	110

CHEVAULEGER REGIMENTS			135-148
Brühl	CL2	1748-64	139
Kurland	CL1	1758-96	135
Prinz Albrecht	CL3	1745-1812	142
Prinz Karl	CL1	1733-58	135
Renard	CL2	1764-78	139
Rutowski	CL4	1742-56	145
Rutowski	CL4	1763-71	145
Sybilski	CL2	1734-48	139

DRAGOON REGIMENTS (1729-1748)			128-134
Arnim	DR3	1745-48	130
Arnstädt	DR1	1732-41	129
Chevalier de Saxe	DR4	1729-41	130
Leipziger	DR2	1733-42	129
Pirch	DR4	1741-44	130
Plötz	DR4	1744-48	130
Rechenberg	DR1	1741-48	129
Schlichting	DR3	1734-45	130
Sondershasusen	DR2	1742-48	129

ENGINEER CORPS	182-183

FREIKORPS	
Freicompagnie Fürst Anhalt	184
Frei-Husaren von Schill Squadron	160

FELDJÄGER	21

GARDE INFANTRY		22-31
1st Garde zu Fuss	1712-48	25
2nd Garde zu Fuss	1712-48	28
Garde zu Fuss	1748-56	25
Grenadier Garde-Regt	1733-43	29
Königliche Leibgarde zu Fuss	1737-43	29
Leib-Grenadier-Garde Regt	1743-56	25
Leib-Grenadier-Garde Bn	1761-63	89
Garde-Grenadier Regt.	1729-33	29
Schweizer Garde		23
Swiss Guard		23

GARDE CAVALRY	32-41
Garde du Corps	33
Karabinier-Garde	39

GENERALS	16-20
Staff officers	19

GRENADIER BNS (1756)	79-90
Gren-Bn Bennigsen [Garde zu Fuss/IR8]	79
Gren-Bn Kavanagh [IR3/IR9]	79
Gren-Bn von de Pforte [IR2/IR7]	79
Gren-Bn von Götze [IR5/IR6]	79
Gren-Bn von Milckau [IR1/Fus]	79
Gren-Bn von Pfundheller [IR4/Leib-Gren-Garde]	79

Saxon Army 1740-1763

Grenadier Bns			79-90
Bellegarde-Grenadiere Bn		1748-50	80
Kurprinzessin-Gren Bn		1750-56	80
[New] Kurprinzessin-Regt		1757	80

Infantry Flags			97-104
M1732 Infantry Flags			97
M1753 Infantry Flags			99
M1758 Infantry Fags			104

Infantry Regiments (1740-56)			43-78
Allnpeck	IR11	1739-48	69
Brühl	IR8	1741-56	63
Du Caila	IR3	1728-40	53
Frankenberg	IR2	1741-44	50
Friese	IR6	1746-55	60
Graf Bellegarde	IR12	1742-48	69
Harthaussen	IR2	1730-41	50
Jasmund	IR10	1746-48	68
Jung Pirch	IR10	1744-46	68
Königin	IR1	1740-56	47
Kosel	IR6	1739-46	60
Lubomirski	IR9	1752-56	65
Minckwitz	IR5	1746-59	58
Neisenmenschel	IR3	1740-46	53
Pirch	IR5	1744-46	58
Prinz Clemens	IR4	1746-56	56
Prinz F. August	IR3	1751-56	54
Prinz Joseph	IR1	1757-63	47
Prinz Maximilian	IR6	1755-56	60
Prinz Xaver	IR7	1733-56	61
Rochow	Fus	1745-56	67
Römer	IR10	1742-44	68
Sachsen-Gotha	IR2	1744-56	50
Schönberg	Fus	1741-45	67
Stollverg-Rosssla	IR9	1742-52	65
Sulkowski	IR5	1734-44	58
Unruh	IR10	1733-42	68
Weissenfels	IR4	1704-46	56

Infantry Regiments (Re-raised 1757-63)			
Block	IR9	1763-78	65
Brühl	IR8	1757-64	63
Kürfurst	IR1	1763-78	47
Lubomirsky	IR9	1757-63	65
Prinz Anton	IR5	1759-1812	58
Prinz Clemens	IR4	1757-1812	56
Prinz F. August	IR3	1757-64	53
Prinz Maximilian	Fus	1758-62	67
Prinz Maximilian	IR6	1757-82	60
Prinz Xaver	IR7	1757-1806	61
Rochow	Fus	1757-58	67
Sachsen-Gotha	IR2	1757-99	50

Prussian IR (Oct 1756-1763)			
Blanckensee	S52	1756-57	25
Flemming	S58	1756-57	56
Friedrich Wilhelm	S59	1756-57	60
Hauss	S55	1757-60	65
Horn	S56	1759-63	53
Jung-Bevern	S57	1756-57	61
Kalckreuth	S56	1758	53
Loen	S56	1756-58	53
Manstein	S53	1756-57	58
Oldenburg	S52	1757	67
Plotho	S54	1758-63	51
Röbel	S55	1760-63	65
Saldern	S54	1756-58	50
Wintersheim	S50	1756-57	67
Wintersheim	S56	1758-59	53
Wylich	S51	1756-57	63

Invalid and Garrison Troops		184-186
Fortress Garrison Officer		185
Henneberg Land Militia		186
Invalid Company		184
Waldheim Invalid Company		184

Kreis Infantry Regs (1733-56)			91-96
Brüchting	Kreis IR4	1733-56	96
Metzradt	Kreis IR2	1733-48	93
Pflugk	Kreis IR2	1748-56	93
Rogucki	Kreis IR3	1742-56	95
Schlichting	Kreis IR1	1733-48	93
Schönberg	Kreis IR3	1756	95
Sternstein	Kreis IR1	1748-56	93
Zschertwitz	Kreis IR3	1733-42	95

Regimental Artillery		178-181
Geachwindück (3- & 6-pdr)	1734-56	178
Gescwinstück in Prussian service	1756-63	180
M1757 4pdr "à la Suédoise"	1758-63	181
Sardinian 4-pdr Quick Fire Gun		181

Sidearms and Weapons	187-188
Carbines	187
Muskets	187
Partizans (Officers)	31, 188
Pistols	47, 187
Polearms (NCOs)	24, 188
Swords	86. 106, 123, 188

Ulan Regiments		149-157
Bertuszewsky-Ulan (Yellow)	1745-68	154
Bielack (Blue)	1762-63	153
Blue Ulan Pulk	1745-63	153
Broninowsky (Red)	1750-57	154
Red Ulan Pulk	1743-63	154
Renard (Red)	1757-59	154
Rudnicki (Blue)	1745-62	153
Schiebel (Red)	1759-63	154
Yellow Ulan Pulk	1745-68	154